THE TEA BOOK

SERENA HARDY

Whittet Books

First published 1979
© 1979 by Serena Hardy
Whittet Books Ltd, The Oil Mills, Weybridge, Surrey

British Library Cataloguing in Publication Data

Hardy, Serena
   The tea book.
   1. Tea
   I. Title
   641.3'37'2   TX415

   ISBN 0-905483-12-X

   ISBN 0–905483–13–8 Pbk

Donatian.

THE TEA BOOK

Contents

Acknowledgments

The publishers would like to thank Mr. R.L. Whittard for his advice on the manuscript; also Mr V.T.H. Parry, Chief Librarian and Archivist of the Royal Botanic Gardens, for permission to photograph the picture on p. 16.

The pictures are reproduced by kind permission of the following: Bantock House Museum: Wolverhampton Art Gallery and Museums, 145; Bodleian Library, 12, 29; British Museum, back jacket, 49, 79; Brooke Bond, 21, 41, 118; Fotomas Index, 47, 52, 71, 74, 78, 89, 96, 116; Foto-Tanjug, 124; Imperial War Museum, 107, 108, 109, 110; Museum of London, 112; National Maritime Museum, 54, 57; Norfolk Museums Service, 13, 121, 143, 144; Popperfoto, 42, 44, 58, 114, 115; Radio Times Hulton Picture Library, 19, 36, 38, 39, 81, 83, 84, 86, 99, 103, 105, 106, 113, 147, 150; Tate Gallery, 77; Tea Board, 15; Tea Council, 20, 22, 23, 24, 25, 26, 27, 28, 92, 117; Twinings, 104; Urasenke Foundation, 17, 65; V & A Museum, front of jacket, 45, 142, 146, 147.

Foreword

Tea is the king and the commoner of all drinks. There is more adventure, and more ritual, surrounding the gathering of tea and its drinking than there is for any other drink. Everyone has very fixed ideas about how the the tea should be made, how it should look, how it should taste. Once made, it is popular all over the world — but in varying amounts. Oddly, it is not the Chinese nor the Indians nor the English who drink, per head of population, the most tea. It is the Irish who claim that record (they drink 3.71 kilos annually each). One tea planter, Robert Fortune, even proposed that the tea plant be grown in 'some warm spot of the south of Ireland'. Another, George Hamilton, said, 'We have Ben Nevis whisky, why not Ben Cruachan tea?'

George Hamilton's comparison of whisky and tea might seem incongruous today, but in his life it seemed good sense. Tea started its career in the West as a favoured aristocrat. It was rare and expensive: an extravagant delicacy. Its costliness is evident from the rich silver tea caddies that now fetch very high prices in the salerooms, and the tiny porcelain teapot, enough for one or two cups, that every lady craved to have. To serve tea was to distribute largesse. Indeed, tea was so snob, so popular, that it necessitated the invention of a whole new meal, also called tea, that quickly and firmly established itself as the most appropriate time for the fashionable ladies to visit each other, to gossip, and to talk about their clothes and their parties, with perhaps the daring diversion of searching for the future in the tea leaves — what a perfect occasion! Henry Fielding well summed up those times: 'Love and scandal are the best sweeteners of tea.'

Tea was too good to stay a rarity and, today, tea's second great attribute is its commonality. Tea is the most catholic, the most forgiving of drinks. Everyone likes a cup of good tea; and a good cup of tea is recognizably the same beverage in virtually every country, even if some peoples do insist on making their tea in rather unusual ways. Indeed, even in England fierce arguments can rage around the question of whether or not to put the tea in first or the milk in first (if you must have milk, you must put it in first; but each to his or her own). Every day huge quantities of tea are drunk in Europe, throughout Asia, in Africa, in America and in Australia. And everywhere it is drunk tea is the epitome of politeness and hospitality: the real cup that cheers. Writing exactly two hundred years after Henry Fielding, Dylan Thomas gave tea one of its highest — if twisted — accolades:

> Here's your arsenic dear.
> And your weedkiller biscuit.
> I've throttled your parakeet.
> I've spat in the vases.
> I've put cheese in the mouseholes.
> Here's your ...
> ... nice tea, dear.

In its progress from fashionable aristocrat to everyday commoner tea has not lost its intricacies of flavour, its subtleties, its fascination. Its great range — from delicate oolongs to rich Assams — can compare with the range of vintage wines; and tea tasters are as fastidious as wine-tasters, detecting almost the hour of the morning the tea leaves were plucked. Just as some people choose wines to suit the food they eat, others choose teas to suit their mood, the time of day, the occasion. For some, quantity is more important than quality — they go so far as to order one-gallon teapots and put tea in their hot-water bottles for midnight swigs (as Gladstone did). In Japan, tea is the basis of a ceremony still practised; the participant must be put in the right frame of mind to appreciate the tea, and his preparation includes a contemplative walk through a Japanese garden. The hordes of visitors to Japan regard the tea ceremony and the Japanese garden to be the twin characteristic sights of the country — and they are not far wrong. Novel support for the business of tea-drinking has come from the recent popularity of herbal teas and other infusions. Tea is rightly regarded as being healthy and refreshing in comparison with coffee — and more interesting too.

The fourth and all-embracing aspect of tea is its central place in the cultures of the countries that adopt it. Whether at a Japanese tea ceremony, in a Bedouin tent, or in an urban café, the preparation and the taking of tea is an essential and characteristic part of society's life. Other drinks — beer, wine, coffee — have had less impact on manners, on hospitality, on the ways in which people come together and drink together. It is not beer that draws people to pubs, but the promise of alcohol; not the drink but the intoxication. Tea, as its lovers know only too well, needs no such lure.

PART I

Lowestoft porcelain teapot, 1761.

1. The Tea Plant and its Cultivation

The tea plant is an evergreen, most of the varieties having glossy leaves with serrated edges and a down-like coating of hair on the underside. Whether growing high into trees, or remaining smaller as bushes, the plant's handsome white flowers with their fragrant smell contrast vividly with the dark leaves, and are instantly recognizable. As a bush, the tea plant resembles the decorative camellia (whose botanical name is *Camellia japonica*) and is in fact of the same family. Both the camellia and the tea plant were first noted by westerners in the Far East in the mid-eighteenth century: the

Tea bush in Assam.

Flower of the tea bush.

camellia in 1727 and the tea plant in 1753. Since then, their paths have diverged: although tea enthusiasts appear to use every possible plant for making tisanes or teas, they have not yet managed to use *Camellia japonica*.

Botanical names are always complex. The full name of the tea plant is *Camellia sinensis (L.) O. Kuntze*. The term *sinensis* is Latin for Chinese, and the name was given because the first tea plant was discovered in China. The 'L.' indicates the Linnaeus system; Linnaeus was a Swedish botanist. O. Kuntze was the botanist who discovered the link between camellias and tea plants. Even botanists find these names confusing: when tea was discovered later in Assam, India, in 1823, some botanists thought they had found a new species, and called the plant *Thea assamica*. But it is now generally agreed that all tea is of the species *Camellia sinensis*. The tea plant is actually indigenous to a vast, fan-shaped area, marked at the north-west by Assam, at the north-east by the China coast and at the southern point by southern Cambodia and Vietnam. The three varieties — China, Assam and Cambodia — correspond with these areas. The China and Assam varieties are now grown throughout the world for their leaves to be made into tea. The Cambodian variety is crossed with others to make hybrids, which are then cultivated. The China plant is hardy, grows in the wild

Rows of tea bushes in Japan so symmetrically shaped that they must have been mechanically plucked.

state to be 9 feet high, and may live as long as 100 years. Its characteristic small leaves produce a delicate tea; when grown on the southern slopes of Mount Everest, the leaves are especially renowned for their flavour. The Assam tree grows much taller, up to 60 feet in the wild, but usually lives only 40 years. There are five different types of Assam: the tender light-leaved, the less tender dark-leaved, the hardy Manipuri, the hardy Burma and the Lushai, which has particularly large leaves, up to a foot long, with a wrinkled surface and prominent veins. All provide a stronger, darker tea than China.

The flowers of all types are about an inch across, with five to seven petals, and delicately scented. Traditionally, they were used to decorate Buddhist temples and the seeds to make tea seed oil (used as a lubricant, also for human consumption). In its natural state, the tea plant is a forest undershrub, and must be cultivated in a suitable soil and climate. Its root system lies mostly in the top three feet of soil; if this topsoil dries out, the plant soon wilts and there is a reduction in growth of leaves. So a moisture-retentive soil is vital. In its normal habitat, the soil would be acid, so all cultivated plants must be grown in acid soil; they will grow happily in clay, sand or peat.

Tea could possibly be grown in Britain or the United States, but the cool climate would produce a small crop, and labour costs would make the product prohibitively expensive. The idea has been suggested, and still appears in some hopeful seed catalogues! Robert Fortune (an important figure in the story of tea, whom we shall meet again later) had suggested growing tea in England back in the 1840s. He wrote:

> Those persons in England who possess tea-plants, and who cultivate them for pleasure, should always bear in mind that, even in the tea districts of China, this shrub will not succeed when planted in low wet land; and this is doubtless one of the reasons why so few persons succeed in growing it in this country. It ought always to be planted on a warm sloping bank, in order to give it a fair chance of success. If some warm spots of this kind in the south of England or Ireland were selected, who knows but our cottagers might be able to grow their own tea? At all events they might have the fragrant herb to look upon.

In the U.S.A. André Michaux, the French botanist, planted tea at Charleston in 1775, but did not remain long enough to see the

Tea cultivation in British India, showing: 1. *Ging Tea Plantation, Darjeeling* 2. *Weighing the leaf* 3. *Plucking the leaf* 4. *Rolling by hand* 5. *Withering in the sun* 6. *Rolling by machinery* 7. *Withering in the factory* 8. *Sorting by machinery*

Planting new tea bushes.

outcome. Also near Charleston in 1845 Dr Julius Smith planted tea, but he died before he saw the results. A Scot named Jackson, who had been a planter in Assam, was sponsored by the Commissioner of Agriculture and set up an experimental tea plantation in Georgia. Samples were even sent to London from here and were judged very fragrant, but no more was heard of the enterprise.

Although hardy by virtue of its deep tap root, which enables it to survive during drought, the tea plant does prefer a humid climate; if the climate is humid, is can also be hot. In 1870 Colonel Money, writing a treatise on tea, said that the climate could not be too hot, as long as the temperature was accompanied by moisture: he observed that a pleasant climate for men cannot be a good one for tea, but, on the other hand, slow growth due to a cool climate at high altitudes often produced a high-quality tea. The accepted figures for temperature are 50°-85° F., and 80-90 inches of rainfall

A tea plucker in India.

per annum, but tea will grow with less rain, and does so in China and Japan.

Tea is usually grown between 1,000 and 7,000 feet above sea-level; the higher it is grown, the more flavour the leaf has, and many of the best teas from Sri Lanka are grown very high. At higher altitudes the plants can suffer from severe frosts, although in Kenya plants are grown above 7,000 feet; and elsewhere have been grown near sea-level. When a tea expert refers to 'high-grown' teas he means they were grown above 4,000 feet; 'mid-grown' between 2,000 and 4,000 feet, and 'low-grown' below 2,000 feet.

Each bush is given about 16 square feet (for the Assam variety; the China needs less space) and is regularly fertilized during the growing season. In Japan huge amounts of nitrogen are used for green tea; the Chinese used to get their black tea without the use of fertilizers. The seeds are seldom used nowadays for the propagation of new plants. Instead, the planter selects plants which have the characteristics he needs, and takes leaf cuttings. He then keeps

Weighing the plucked leaf in India.

Withering vats.

the plant to a height of about three feet for easy harvesting; by continual plucking of the leaves and occasional pruning, the production of flowers is retarded and leaves are encouraged.

The leaf is always plucked in the same way, by removing the bud and a few leaves (usually two) at the end of the shoot. Leaves that have not developed fully and do not have the characteristic serrations are called 'fish leaves'. They indicate that the plant is going through the *banjhi* or resting phase that alternates with the 'flushes' or growth phases. The tea plant 'flushes' during its growing season at regular intervals. The times of the flushes depend on the climate. In South India and Sri Lanka the growing season continues all the year round, with the best teas being produced during December and January in India, and in the earlier part of the year in Sri Lanka. However, because of monsoons, cropping is not continuous in Sri Lanka; plucking at any time is either in the East or West. In Africa, plucking goes on all through the year. In

Rolling the leaf in India.

North India and China there are seasons for tea, being mainly April to October, with the best teas being at the end of the season, with the cooler weather, and in China the best coming in the early part of the year. In the Dooars (India) some autumnal teas of September and October have a special flavour and character that fetches high prices.

Ever since Robert Fortune investigated Chinese tea growing in the nineteenth century, the experts have been ready with detailed prescriptions for the correct method of plucking a tea bush. There have been many fashions, nowadays helped by scientific research. The Chinese used to strip the plant annually; the later Assam plantations followed this example until 1853 when George Williamson left most of the spring growth on his plants in order to strengthen them and produced a better yield.

In 1870 Colonel Money wrote an explanation of the behaviour of the plants when pruned or plucked. Pruning, he pointed out, promotes growth during the period of recovery while the plant replaces lost foliage. It is from the unopened leaves and the youngest leaves that tea is manufactured. So the more buds that are allowed to grow, the greater the amount of tea to be gathered. The reason for the Chinese method of stripping the tree is probably that their leaves grow in harder conditions, with a limited season, smaller leaves and lower vitality, so the tree's vitality is restricted naturally.

Tea plucking is a labour-intensive operation, and usually done by women, except in Africa. One person can pick a maximum of about 77 lb. of leaves in a day, which would make up 20 lb. of black tea. A pound of manufactured tea may require as many as 3,000 shoots (comprising 2 leaves and a bud), so, even working a 10-hour day, a woman would have to pick 100 shoots a minute to attain the target. During the season, the tea bush may be plucked as often as every five days, and the work force needed is enormous. It is obvious that labour makes up a large proportion of the cost of tea. Since labour is so expensive in the developed world, tea growing remains concentrated in Third World countries. There have been many attempts to mechanize plucking. The Georgian estates in the U.S.S.R. use plucking machines which date back to the mid-nineteen thirties. The Japanese have devised cunning shears with

Firing the leaf in Kenya.

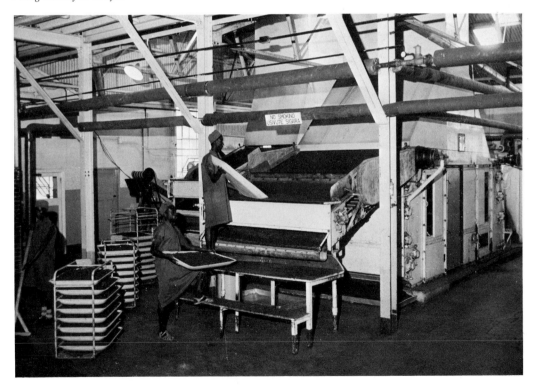

pouches attached to the blades, enabling 300 lb. of leaf to be gathered by one labourer in a day. Others have been tried in India, Sri Lanka and East Africa, but it is generally agreed that machines cannot discriminate sufficiently to select the bud and first two leaves for plucking, and therefore do not have any advantages over hand plucking. Machines also require more space to be left between bushes.

The greatest amount of work in making tea lies in the cultivation of the plant and the plucking of the leaf. But manufacturing is just as expert. The leaf is withered, rolled, fermented, fired and sorted — processes that require no less skill, but are increasingly being mechanized. It is these later stages that partly determine what kind of tea — black, green or oolong — will result. Black is 'fermented', green is 'unfermented' and oolong is 'semi-fermented'. Oolong is only made from the Chinese variety, whereas black and green can be made from China, Assam or Cambodian.

Grading tea in India.

Tea is manufactured near the tea garden because it must be made from freshly plucked leaves (preferably not more than a few hours old). Black tea is plucked on a clear morning when the dew has just evaporated. Small producers in Japan used to leave the tea leaves exposed to the sun for at least an hour; then lightly roll them to develop a red colour and aroma, heat them in an iron pan, roll and heat a few more times, and finally dry them in a basket over a charcoal fire.

In large-scale operations, the leaves are dried artificially for a complete day in temperatures of 80°-90°F. so that one third of the moisture of the leaves is lost. The withering prepares the leaf for rolling, which releases the juices and enzymes that go to make the characteristic flavour of black tea. The old method of rolling by feet has now disappeared, and now most rolling is mechanized. A Rotorvane machine is used for the rolling, and the coarser leaves are then cut, torn and curled (C.T.C.) in another machine. Black tea is defined by the fermentation process that then takes place: the rolled leaf is spread out in a cool, humid atmosphere for about three hours; the main chemical change that takes place is the oxidation of the 'polyphenols' (which impart flavour). The leaf also turns coppery in colour. Finally the tea is fired, which produces its black colour. Firing can be in pans or baskets over a fire, as in the old days in China, but nowadays most factories do the firing by passing hot air through the tea. Black tea is strong in flavour, and is the tea usually preferred in the U.K. and Ireland.

Oolong is made from a special type of the China tea plant: *chesima*. It is then prepared in the same way as black tea, and may later be flavoured with jasmine, orange or lemon. These flavoured teas are very popular in the United States.

In China and Japan, green tea is preferred: it has a fresher flavour, and is drunk without milk. To make green tea, the leaf is given more initial heating or steaming, in order to stabilize it. The enzymes are made inactive; the leaf is then hand-rolled, and no fermentation takes place. It is then further heated or roasted; throughout the product remains a greenish colour.

When the leaves are ready for selling, they are sorted for size and packed. Tea that is exported or stored for some time must be treated with special care, as tea can go off. Since it is hygroscopic (i.e. it absorbs water) tea must be kept in airtight containers, and is always fired (i.e. dried out) before being packed. In the early days, the long journey to Europe meant that the delicate flavour was often spoiled by mould or damp. Unseasoned wooden chests had a

Packing and sealing tea-chests in India.

bad reputation for imparting an unpleasant cheesey flavour. The first tea from Assam, which arrived in London in November 1838 had a most awkward journey. It had been re-fired in Calcutta (to dry it for the journey) and loaded on a ship together with smelly ox-hides; to prevent contamination, the tea-chests were soldered into tin cases and given a cabin to themselves. Edward Money in 1878 had strong words to say about packing:

> By far the best Tea boxes are the teak ones made at Rangoon. The wood is impervious to insects of all kinds, even white ants. Sawn by machinery the pieces sent to compose each box are very regular. The plank is half inch and each chest made up measures inside 23 by 18 by 18½ inches, and necessarily outside 24 by 19 by 19½ inches. The inner cubical contents are 7,659 cubic inches, and this suffices for above one maund* of fine, and under a maund of coarse Tea.

* A maund is 80 lb.

These Rangoon chests came as a kit, which included lead sheets for the lining and some silver foil to go on top of the tea. By the 1890s machinery had been developed to agitate the tea-chest so that tea could be packed more densely, so replacing the traditional method of rocking the tea-chest on a split bamboo cane and trampling the tea under foot. Various woods and metals were tried, but plywood proved most suitable, and when lead was suspected by the American authorities of poisoning, aluminium foil was substituted. Nowadays, tea-chests, like pots and caddies (see Chapter 12), are almost as familiar in their own right as the leaf they contain.

Doloi Tea Garden, Sylhet, India.

DOLOI GARDEN TEA FACTORY.

Rolling is the next operation which the leaf undergoes. This is still done **in China by the hands and feet of sometimes very dirty natives**; and when we mention that this operation is now all done in Doloi, as in most other Tea Gardens in India, by machinery, we make a statement which **must strongly recommend Indian Teas** to all.

Fermentation which comes next, is not always necessary, for Green Tea is unfermented; however all Doloi Teas are prepared for this market—where Green Teas are not in demand—and go through the process of fermentation. It is here that

CAREFUL WATCHING

great judgment, and much experience are required, and where a manager who thoroughly understands his business is necessary. Fermentation changes the leaf from green to brown, and develops the aroma.

Drying comes next. It is done by the new down draught Tea Dryer, which is coming into general use in India and Ceylon. During drying the surface of the leaf becomes darker, although the interior still retains a high rich brown colour. The Chinese still adhere to their old system of drying over small charcoal fires.

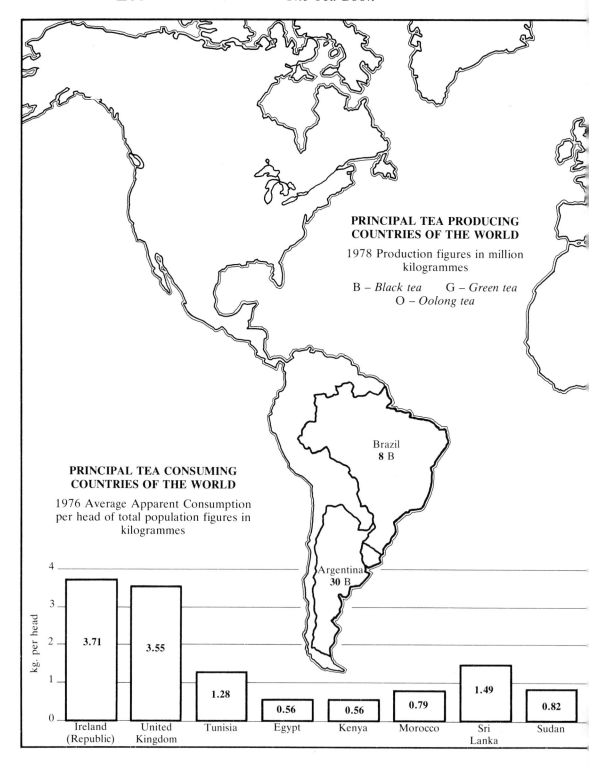

**PRINCIPAL TEA PRODUCING
COUNTRIES OF THE WORLD**

1978 Production figures in million
kilogrammes

B – *Black tea*   G – *Green tea*
O – *Oolong tea*

Brazil
8 B

Argentina
30 B

**PRINCIPAL TEA CONSUMING
COUNTRIES OF THE WORLD**

1976 Average Apparent Consumption
per head of total population figures in
kilogrammes

kg. per head

Ireland (Republic)	United Kingdom	Tunisia	Egypt	Kenya	Morocco	Sri Lanka	Sudan
3.71	3.55	1.28	0.56	0.56	0.79	1.49	0.82

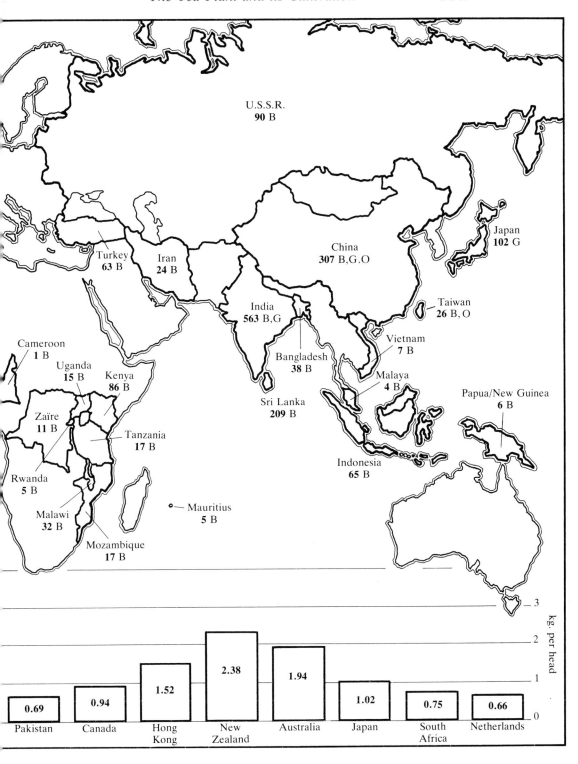

U.S.S.R.
90 B

Japan
102 G

China
307 B,G,O

Turkey
63 B

Iran
24 B

India
563 B,G

Taiwan
26 B, O

Vietnam
7 B

Bangladesh
38 B

Malaya
4 B

Cameroon
1 B

Uganda
15 B

Kenya
86 B

Sri Lanka
209 B

Papua/New Guinea
6 B

Zaïre
11 B

Tanzania
17 B

Rwanda
5 B

Indonesia
65 B

Malawi
32 B

Mauritius
5 B

Mozambique
17 B

kg. per head

Pakistan	Canada	Hong Kong	New Zealand	Australia	Japan	South Africa	Netherlands
0.69	0.94	1.52	2.38	1.94	1.02	0.75	0.66

2. The Cup that Cheers

List of Teas

Remember that 'high-grown' implies a good flavour, followed by 'medium-grown' and then 'low-grown'.

Most teas sold under the name of a place of origin are nowadays blended with teas from other regions. In this list, we have included both proprietary names of tea that can be found on sale in shops and also names of regions that provide tea; where the latter are self-drinkers, we have indicated so.

Black teas are usually drunk with milk, at least in Britain, and also in New Zealand and Australia. But in many other countries black tea is used in smaller quantities and the liquor drunk without milk. Some fine flavoured black teas, such as some China and Ceylons, are perfectly drinkable without milk even when made strong. Ultimately, the addition of milk is a matter of personal preference. However, it is not usually recommended to add milk to green or oolong tea.

Name	*Origin*	*Leaf*	*Characteristics*
Assam	North India	Hard, flinty, grey-black; bright gold tips in high grades.	Rich, heavy tea, pungent and strong; almost too strong on its own, used in blending.
Brick Tea	China, Russia	Compressed. Can be black or green.	Not usually a quality tea.
Cachar	North India	Grey-black.	Thick sweet liquor, not so strong as Assam. Mostly used in blends.

Name	Origin	Leaf	Characteristics
Ceylon	Sri Lanka	Black, neat and even, with good proportion of tips in best qualities.	High-grown some of the best tea in the world; some are self-drinker teas, with strong, full, round taste and delicate flavour. Sometimes sold by districts.
China Caravan	China	Black	Blend of Keemun and perhaps oolong to imitate the tea that went by camel.
Ching Wo	China	Black: tightly rolled, silky.	Copper-coloured liquor, delicate aroma, strong and flavoury.
Chunmee	China	Green	Sweet and pungent; very little colour.
Coronation Tea	Blend	Black	Character of Ceylon teas but strength of Assam.
Darjeeling	North India	Black: large leaf qualities usually best flavour.	High-grown; some of finest of India teas; self-drinker, rich flavour and exquisite bouquet reminiscent of muscatel.
Dikoya	Sri Lanka	Black	Full, round and sweet. High-grown, very good quality, mostly used in blends. Rarely a self-drinker.
Dimbula	Sri Lanka	Black	High-grown; one of the best.
Dooars	North India	Black	Low-grown; strong colour and full-bodied taste, softer than Assams.
Earl Grey	China	Black	Blended tea flavoured with the oil from the peel of bergamot.
English Breakfast	North China	Black	Originally blended North China Congous; now usually Assam plus a little Ceylon. Strong, full-bodied, fragrant and sweet.
Formosa Oolong	Taiwan	Oolong; large greenish-brown leaf. The best have silver tips.	The best of these are some of the great teas of the world; a natural, slightly peachy flavour. Straw-coloured liquor.
Gunpowder	China Taiwan	Green; young leaves, tippy, rolled in balls ranging from Pin Head to Pea Leaf.	Fruity flavour; gunpowder is best grade of China green tea.
Hunan (Oonam)	China	Black	Bright coloured liquor; smoky flavour. Best known growth called Oonfa. Rarely found on sale.

Name	Origin	Leaf	Characteristics
Hyson	China	Green; small, well-made curly leaf; older than Imperial and young Hyson.	Dated name for green tea no longer in use.
I-Chang	China	Black; small leaf.	Rich, full-bodied, with metallic, slightly smoky flavour.
Imperial	China	Green; large, round, rolled leaf; older than Hyson.	Good quality grade.
Indonesia	Indonesia Java/Sumatra	Black	High-quality teas, comparable with Ceylon.
Irish Breakfast	India	Black, with a blaze of golden tips.	Blend of Assam teas; strong, full.
Jasmine	China	Green or a mix of black and green containing jasmine flowers.	Flavoured with jasmine. Do not add milk.

Java — *see* Indonesia

Name	Origin	Leaf	Characteristics
Kanan Devan	South India	Black	Similar to Ceylon tea, with rounded, but delicate flavour.
Keemun	China	Black	A North China Congou, with clear coloured liquor, smooth, sweet taste and aroma like an orchid. The best of the China blacks.
Kenya	Kenya	Black	High-grown are as good as high-grown Ceylon teas; all have good flavour, some lack strength. Mostly used in blending.
Lady Londonderry	India, Sri Lanka, Taiwan	Black	Made for a famous hostess at the beginning of the century; a blend.
Lapsang Souchong	China	Black	Full-bodied, rich, with strong, smoky, tarry taste. Very little required to flavour a blend or for infusions.
Lemon	Various	Black	Flavoured with lemon essence and sometimes lemon peel.
Limeflower	Various	Black or green	Scented with lime. Blend of black teas.
Malaysia	Malaysia	Black	Comparable with Ceylons and Indonesians, usually blended.
Moyune	China	Green; greyish leaf.	One of best China green teas, subtle flavour like cowslips.

Name	Origin	Leaf	Characteristics
Nilgiris	South India	Black	At the right season fine, flavoury teas, with brisk, pungent flavour, slightly like Ceylons.
Ningchow	China	Black; greyish leaf.	North China Congou; good, clear.
North China Congou	China	Black	'Burgundy' of tea.
Nuwara Eliya	Sri Lanka	Black	High-grown, quality tea.
Orange Pekoe — can also be a grading for any teas.			
Orange Pekoe	China	Black	Highly scented Souchong, used for blending to lend jasmine flavour.
Pakling	China	Black	One of best South China Congous; clear, but thin liquor.
Paklum	China	Black; small; neatly made.	Pleasant, but thin flavour.
Panyong	China	Black	Delicate and flavoury; full-bodied and with character.
Pouchong	China, Taiwan	Oolong	Scented with gardenia, jasmine or yulan blossom. The China pouchong has a brighter taste. Formosa a duller flavour.
Rose	Various	Black	Blends scented with rose petals.
Rose Congou	China	Black	Mixed with rose petals.
Russian Caravan	China	Black	North China Congous; flavour to imitate camel caravan tea.
Russian	Russia	Black	Sometimes called Georgian Tea. Coloury, plain tea.
Seychelles Tea	Seychelles	Black	Ordinary liquor; reputed to be unpolluted and fresh.
Souchong	China	Black; large leaf.	Rich, syrupy.
South China Congou	China	Black; reddish leaf.	High-quality teas; 'clarets'.
String Tea	China	Oolong	A less fermented grade of tea.
Sumatra — *see* Indonesia			
Sylhet	Bangladesh	Black; neat leaf.	Coloury liquor. Mostly blended.
Tarry Lapsang	China Taiwan	Black	Tarry flavour.
Terai	North India	Black; small leaf.	Soft liquor, tasting remotely like poor Darjeeling.

Name	Origin	Leaf	Characteristics
Travancore	South India	Black	Similar to Ceylon Tea.
Twankey	China	Green	Older grade of green tea, not seen any more.
Uganda	Uganda	Black	High-grown, less quality than Kenya. Used only for blending.
Vanilla	Various	Black	Flavoured with vanilla.
Yamashiro	Japan	Green	Most sought-after of Japan teas.
Young Hyson	China	Green; long, rough, twisted leaf.	Grade of green tea. No longer seen.
Yunnan	China	Black, often with tips.	Sweet aroma, strong, thick liquor, sappy taste.

Teas can vary greatly, from dark infusions to light golden, from tarry to cowslip flavour. The uniformity of packet blends of tea has not encouraged experimentation with different kinds of tea;

Tea-tasting at Grocers Exhibition, Islington, in 1936.

perhaps this chapter will provide some encouragement. The differences in flavour and appearance are caused not so much by the three varieties of tree (China, Assam and Cambodia) as by climate, soil and method of manufacture. Describing flavours is a frustrating task (perfumers have the same stuttering incoherence when smelling a perfume and rose-growers, when faced with a new hybrid). Tea experts, however, have evolved their own evocative language to describe the flavours of tea, some of which are:

Brassy

Brisk (a lively taste, similar to fresh soda water compared with stale)

Fishy

Flat or soft (opposite of 'brisk')

Flavoury (a distinctive taste)

Full

Grassy

Harsh (a raw, bitter taste, with little strength)

Insipid

Malty (with a faint taste of malt, found in well-fired quality teas)

Metallic

Raw/green (bitter)

Rich

Smoky (a taste of smoke, desirable in some China teas)

Toasty

A tea connoisseur will also look at the leaf. Again, expertise has built up around colour, size and shape. For a green tea, a yellow-gold leaf is preferable. An open, flat leaf infuses more quickly than a tightly twisted one, which will give a better second cup. The expert will also smell the tea, and inspect and smell the liquor to see if it is bright and clear, and whether it 'creams', which means that a milky film rises to the top of the cup and indicates a strong, rich tea. He will describe that sensation when tasting tea of roughness in the mouth (so helpful in the early morning) as 'pungency' (a virtue, not a vice), and his greatest praise will go to a 'brisk, full, rich, flavoury' tea.

Most of the names of teas reflect the traditional names of the areas where they were grown (though nowadays, all the tea in the blend may no longer come from that area), e.g. Darjeeling, Formosa Oolong, Ceylon. (The names of the places have changed now too.) The black tea-growing areas are India, Bangladesh, Sri Lanka, China, Java and Sumatra in modern Indonesia, and other new tea-producing areas such as Nepal, the Seychelles, Africa and

Liptons tea advertisement.

South America. The main green tea areas are China and Japan, while oolongs are produced in Taiwan and Fukien province in China.

Few tea-drinkers would not agree that Ceylon teas are some of the world's best. The black, high-grown teas from this colourful island (suitably renamed 'Sri Lanka', an ancient name for Ceylon meaning 'lord of lands', in 1972) when harvested at certain times of the year have a delicious, delicate flavour and can be drunk on their own. Ceylon teas harvested at other times are used for blending; they soften and give colour to pungent Assams, for example. Some of the 'cold-weather' Ceylons used in small quantities have such pungent flavour that a small proportion adds character and flavour to a blend. The grading system in Sri Lanka begins at the top with 'Orange Pekoe' then goes on 'Pekoe', 'Pekoe Souchong', 'Broken Pekoe Souchong', 'Broken Orange Pekoe', 'Broken Pekoe', 'Fannings' and 'Dust' (which is not as bad as it sounds). The grading only refers to the appearance of the leaf, however, and does not necessarily imply good flavour; 'Orange Pekoe', which has acquired a reputation for quality in the West, is really misunderstood. Just to confuse you further, 'Orange Pekoe' can also refer to a scented China tea.

Because of its size, India produces a vast range of different teas; it has some green tea, of relatively poor quality, and most of the best India tea is black. Of the teas grown in the north-east of India, the Assams and Darjeelings are most significant. Assams are grown in the Brahmaputra valley, and they make full, thick, rich

U.K. Tea Company advertisement.

tea so strong that they are normally blended with thinner teas. Darjeeling tea has a distinctive, delightful flavour. Its location may be the cause — it is grown high along the Himalayas at heights up to 6,500 feet. Pure Darjeeling is the most expensive tea of India. It is so good, it can be drunk on its own, without blending: what the trade calls a 'self-drinker'. Its flavour is often described as being like Muscat grapes, or blackcurrants, and its liquor is full-bodied, rich and red. Once tasted, the best Darjeelings are never to be forgotten. Sadly, the best qualities fetch the highest prices of all teas in Calcutta auctions, and they are exported to Russia and the Gulf States, rarely to Britain or the U.S. Anyway, not many of us could afford to drink unmixed Darjeeling. Other notable teas from the same area are the Dooars.

At the southern end of India, the teas are more similar to the Sri Lankan teas: the best are from Anamalai, Nilgiris, Travancore.

China, like India, produces both green and black teas of great variety. It also produces oddities like brick tea, tablet tea, ball and faggot tea, but these are mainly popular in Russia, Tibet and in China itself. The familiar western black teas are usually divided into North China and South China Congous. What used to be called 'English Breakfast Tea' was North China Congou; these teas are aromatic, full-bodied and sweet. W.H. Ukers, who compared the flavours of tea to those of wine in his *All About Tea* (1935) likened the North China Congous to a good burgundy. The highest quality teas are the Keemuns, Ningchows and Ichangs, and they are among the best teas to come from China. His 'clarets' are the South China Congous with a totally different flavour; the best of these are the Paklums, Panyongs and Paklings. 'Souchong' is a generic term for the large leaf of most Congous, but is also applied to the large-leaf grades from India, Sri Lanka, Sumatra, etc. Souchong teas from China have a rich, syrupy, slightly smoky liquor, the best of which are Lapsang Souchongs.

China green teas are graded from 'Gunpowder' at the top, through 'Imperial', 'Hyson' and 'Twankey' to 'Dust'. In this case, the grades refer to age, with 'Gunpowder' being the youngest, and therefore the best. One of the best of the China green teas is Moyune, which has a delightful cowslip flavour. Other teas from China include the oolongs, of which Foochow is the best, and the scented teas, of which Foochow Scented Orange Pekoe is one of the best. Another is Canton Scented Orange Pekoe (again, do not get confused with the Ceylon tea grades here, which also include 'Orange Pekoe'), which produces a strong, flavoury tea.

Modern tea-tasting.

Japan produces almost exclusively green tea, and most is drunk domestically. To continue with the wine analogy, the Japanese green teas would be the 'white wines' with delicate, light flavours. As with the China green teas, they are graded by age, the youngest being the best. (The reverse of some wines!) Tea is further classified by the method of making it into *sencha* (the tea of commerce), *tencha* (ceremonial tea), *bancha* (low-grade tea for home use) and *gyokuro* (made from bushes which have been shaded). The most sought-after teas come from Yamashiro, near Kyoto, the old capital of Japan.

Taiwan is famous for its oolongs, which must be the 'champagnes' of teas. They are deliciously pungent, with a fruity flavour. Taiwan also produces what are called 'three-quarter fermented' teas, 'Flowery Orange Pekoe', 'Orange Pekoe' and 'Pekoe', and a scented oolong, called 'Pouchong', with gardenia or jasmine.

It is rare and expensive nowadays to get one of these teas which has not been blended. Even a 'self-drinker', like Darjeeling or Ceylon, will usually have been blended before it arrives in the shop in a packet. Nowadays, blending goes on behind the scenes at the tea companies, but in Victorian and Edwardian days, the housewife would blend her own tea, or have it specially blended at the grocer. Grocers proudly announced themselves as 'Tea Blender and Provision Merchant'. The main reasons for blending are to reduce the price of the more expensive teas, to even out variations in quality in teas, and the undeniable fact that many teas are not worth drinking on their own. The skill of the blender is consistently to choose teas that will, when blended, conform to the character of the 'brand' of tea. For each brand he will follow an established brand recipe. He may, for instance, blend an Assam tea, which will

A Tibetan making 'butter' tea: yak butter, salt, tea and boiling water are churned together.

provide a full-bodied liquor, with a Darjeeling, which will provide a good flavour. China black tea, which is not so dominating as Assam, blends well with a fine Ceylon tea. Blending is directed at particular markets; the Irish, for instance, are agreed to have good taste in tea, and they tend to choose blends with a high proportion of tips and which are strong, rich and pungent.

What makes tea taste the way it does? The consensus seems to point towards something called 'polyphenols', which are related to tannin. The aroma comes from the natural oils in the leaf, and its stimulating properties come from caffeine. The link between a high concentration of polyphenols and a good flavour has been proved: there are more polyphenols in the young and slower-growing leaves, which have traditionally been highly prized. In the manufacture of black tea, the polyphenols are oxidized, whereas for green tea the oxidation is retarded. As for the diet-conscious, tea is a heaven-sent drink in terms of calories; it contains a slim 4 calories per cup (a figure which is hugely enlarged by the addition of milk and sugar).

Although the addition of milk to black and many other teas is a matter of taste — and fiercely debated — its addition to green or oolong teas is sacrilege. The most important ingredient in tea is the water used; hard and soft waters give completely different results, but artificially softened water is not recommended. Well water is not as brisk and lively as running water, as Tung Po said:

> Take water from a running stream and boil it over a lively fire; that from springs in the hills is the best and river-water the next, while well-water is the worst. A lively fire is a clear and bright charcoal fire. When making an infusion, do not boil the water too hastily, as first it begins to sparkle like crab's eyes, then somewhat like fish's eyes, and lastly it boils up like pearls innumerable, springing and waving about.

An elegant rebuke to those people who let the kettle boil for ten minutes before they make the tea.

The traditional way of making tea in the West is well-known:

1. Use a good quality tea.
2. Warm the pot.
3. Use a teaspoonful of tea per person and one for the pot.
4. Bring freshly drawn mains water to the boil.
5. As soon as the water boils, take the teapot to the kettle and pour in the boiling water.

Moujik family of U.F.A. seated around a samovar.

6. Stir, and let the tea infuse for not less than five minutes; longer for some teas.
7. Put milk into the cup, if desired.
8. Pour in the tea and adjust milk and sugar to taste.

But others would regard this method as barbaric. The Russians drink their tea with jam, or suck it through sugar lumps. The Eskimos make theirs by throwing some tea into the kettle, boiling for ten minutes and then serving. The Tibetans chip their tea off a block or brick, put it into cold water and then boil it for some hours until it is thick and black. To western tastes the result is a revolting stew, but then the Tibetans add salt or soda and strain the liquid off into a cylindrical container; next some butter is added, the mixture is churned vigorously, and then served in little bowls. Would you perhaps prefer 'letpet tea', which the Burmese drink, and which the Thais call 'miyang'? Green tea leaves are steamed and kneaded and then pressed into six-foot deep pits. After some weeks there, the leaves are rescued, washed in brine and eaten as a salad, with garlic, oil and prawns. The Koreans drop tea leaves into boiling water and then serve them with raw eggs and rice cakes. The Mongols make their tea from brick tea, boiled in water with fat and salt. It is then strained, and made into a kind of soup with milk, butter and roasted flour. If these suggestions do not appeal, we include in Chapter 11 some other suggestions for cooking tea, cooking with tea and cooking for tea.

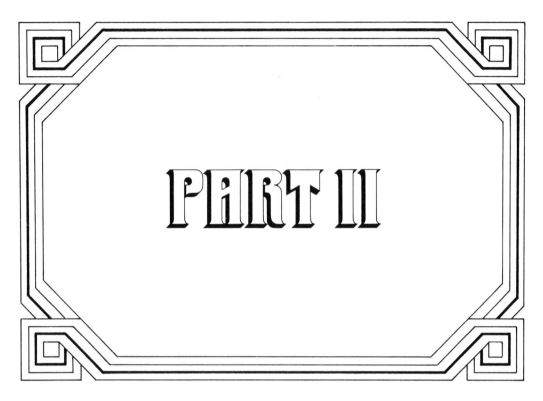

PART II

London hallmarked silver stand and kettle, 1705–6.

3. All the Tea in China

The Chinese, proving yet again their long history of civilization, have many stories about tea being first drunk as long ago as 2700 B.C. One story of how they discovered it celebrates the Emperor Shen-Nung, in 2737 B.C. (about the time Noah was casting off in the Ark). The Emperor, being a hygienic man, was boiling his

The Emperor of China arrives to meet Lord Macartney. Engraving by G. Nicol from picture by William Alexander.

drinking water when he noticed leaves falling into the water from a branch on the fire. He discovered that the leaves imparted a delightful flavour to his water; apparently they came from the wild tea tree. Another story credits an old lady of the T'sin Dynasty (255-206 B.C.) with selling tea in the market from a miraculous cup that never emptied. She distributed the money to beggars and orphans, but was for some obscure reason thrown into prison, whence she escaped by flying out of the window, clutching the cup in her hand.

Until the T'ang Dynasty (famous for its pottery horses), tea was drunk as a medicine or stimulant, a remedy for 'noxious gases of the body, and as a cure for lethargy'. To fulfil the demand, trees growing naturally were cut down and then stripped of their leaves. Such destruction of the wild trees threatened to eradicate them, so, for the first time, tea plants were specially grown and cultivated. Legends relate that monkeys were used in the early days to gather the tea leaves that grew at the tops of trees. Around A.D. 620 tea began to be appreciated as a beverage drunk for pleasure. By A.D. 780 it had become such big business that the tea merchants commissioned a writer, Lu Yu, to write the first treatise on tea, a three-volume, ten-part work entitled *Cha Ching* (Tea Classic). Lu Yu gives the following instructions for processing the leaves:

> All the tea is gathered in the second, third and fourth moons; the leaves must not be gathered in rainy, or even in cloudy weather, but when it is fair and clear. Bruise and pat them with the hands, roast them over a fire, pack and close them up. In this manner tea is prepared, and there are a thousand and ten thousand different kind.

After eulogizing at length on fragrance and flavour, he writes that: 'Tea tempers the spirit and harmonizes the mind; dispels lassitude and relieves fatigue; awakens thought and prevents drowsiness; lightens and refreshes the body and clears the perceptive faculties.' Lu Yu tells us that tea was universal in some parts of Honan, Shensi, Hunan and Szechwan; that there were then three kinds of tea — ordinary, ground and cake tea, which was put in a jar or bottle after being pounded. He says that tea was sometimes flavoured with onion, ginger, ju-jube, orange peel and peppermint, but rejects this as 'the slop water of the ditch'.

In the ninth century an Arab merchant, Soliman, visited China and wrote that tea was the common beverage of the country: 'the infusion preserves them from all distempers'. Whipped tea soon made its appearance; the dried leaf was ground to a powder and whipped in hot water with a whisk (in a similar manner to that used in the Japanese tea ceremony). Elaborate tea houses appeared in many cities and tea was cultivated widely, the best, destined to become an important export, was grown in the south-eastern parts of the country.

It was some time later that Europe began to learn of the new drink. Turkish caravans had begun trading on the northern borders of China at the end of the fifth century, and at the beginning of the sixth Tartars had taken tea from China to the Arabs and Persians. During the Sung Dynasty (A.D. 960-1127) the Chinese Government permitted a regular export trade on the northern border, which developed into the caravan trade across the Mongolian

A surfeit of tea?

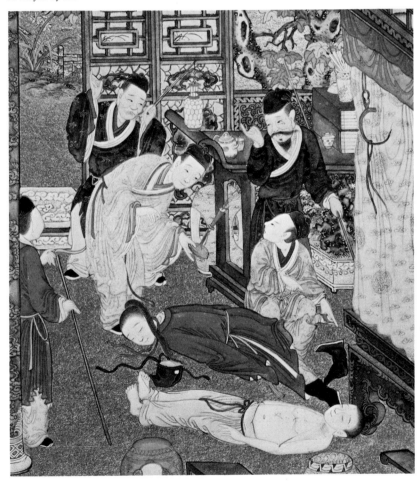

Desert and gave the name to the 'caravan' teas. Simultaneously, in the South of China the trade with Tibet began in its curious form — brick tea. But the delights of tea really remained hidden from the West until the sixteenth century, when Portuguese mariner Vasco da Gama sailed round the Cape of Good Hope into the Indian Ocean (1497). For his achievement, the Portuguese were given a Papal Bull granting them a trading monopoly to the East. But, Pope or no Pope, the Portuguese were only able to establish themselves on the periphery of China, at Macao. Early Portuguese contributions to the tea trade were mainly literary: more words about tea than tea itself. One of the best-known writers was Linschooten, who had been secretary to the Portuguese Archbishop of Goa from 1583-9. His book *Itinerario* was published in 1596. The following quotation (from the English translation made soon after) is typical of many of the descriptions of this strange new beverage:

> Everie man hath a table alone, without tablecloths or napkins, and eateth with two pieces of wood like the men of China; they drinke wine of Rice, wherewith they drinke themselves drunke, and after their meat use a certain drinke, which is a pot of hote water, which they drink as hote as ever they may endure, whether it be Winter or Summer ... the aforesaid warme water is made with the powder of a certaine hearbe called CHAA, which is much esteemed, and is well accounted of among them and all such as of any countenance or habilitie have the said water kept for them in a secret place, and the gentlemen make it themselves; and when they will entertaine any of their friends, they give him some of the warme water to drinke; for the pots wherein they sieth it, and wherein the hearbe is kept, with the earthen cups which they drink it in, they esteeme as much of them as we doe of Diamants, Rubies and other precious stones, and they are not esteemed for their newness, but for their oldness, and for that they are made by a good workman.

However, it was not the Portuguese but the Dutch who took advantage of those travellers' tales and became most enthusiastic about the oriental novelty. When Portugal, which had been bringing tea back from China, closed its ports to the Dutch in 1595, the Dutch were forced to find their trade elsewhere. They soon became well established in Bantam in Java (renamed Batavia); and also in Japan. Although the first tea to arrive in Europe (probably green tea) came via Bantam, it is not certain whether it had originated in China or Japan. Anyway, back in Holland, it quickly caught on as a medicine. The Dutch claimed it had laxative powers. They re-exported it to Portugal, France and Italy, where it was sold by apothecaries as a remedy for all kinds of ills. When Catherine of Braganza, the young Infanta, married Charles II of England, she brought her tea-drinking with her and helped to popularize the drink.

However, the reaction of the Chinese to the western traders was not welcoming. Russia, trading by land rather than by sea, had considerably more success. Rumours of the new drink of tea arrived in Moscow in 1567, brought by two Cossacks, Ivan Petroff and Boornash Yalysheff. The Chinese were even so forthcoming as to send a gift of tea to Czar Alexis in 1618. A trade agreement was made in 1689 (the Nerchinsk Treaty) and soon regular caravans were bringing tea through Mongolia and Siberia. At first the Russian Government controlled the caravans, but after 1835, when the Empress Elizabeth established an open trade, private caravans went. They consisted of 200-300 camels, each loaded with 4 chests (about 600 lb.) of tea. It was a slow procession. The camels walked only $2\frac{1}{2}$ miles per hour, and the journey was 11,000 miles long. Most trips took 16 months. The caravan trade reached its height in 1860-80, when the Siberian Railway was built, and business transferred to that. In the middle of the nineteenth century the Russians started buying brick tea in Hankow, and later built their own brick tea factories there.

It was a harder battle for other European countries to get into China and trade with her. The attitude of the Chinese to the merchants was arrogant and dismissive — xenophobic in the extreme. The officials of the Celestial Empire did not hesitate to use their powers to prevent the western traders, whom they regarded as barbarians, from gaining any established rights or connections. A few official missions or embassies did gain entry and found themselves the beneficiaries of the deeply rooted and all-embracing customs that constitute Chinese hospitality. But once the embassy had departed, the relationships between Chinese and European continued to be hostile.

In 1637 the directors of the Dutch East India Company advised their governor general in Batavia that: 'As tea begins to come into use by some of the people, we expect jars of Chinese as well as Japanese tea with each ship.' The Dutch were especially keen. They even succeeded in dispatching an embassy to the Chinese Emperor in 1655. Jean Nieuhoff described how the 'barbarians'

Loading tea junks at Tsen-tang at the end of the nineteenth century.

were allowed as far as the gates of Canton and were there feasted by their imperial host. His account is also interesting as it is the first reference to drinking tea with milk (the exception rather than the norm in China):

> At the beginning of the dinner, there were served several bottles of The or tea, served to the table, wherof they drank to the Embassadors, bidding them welcome: This drink is made of the Herb The or Cha in fair water, which afterwards they boil until a third part be consumed, to which they adde warm milk about a forth part, with a little salt, and then drink it as hot as they can well endure.

England was also trying to open the door to China. The earliest mention of tea in the records of the East India Company is the request by a Mr Wickham in Japan to his colleague Mr Eaton in Macao 'for a pot of the best sort of chaw'. In 1637 the British made a forceful — and ultimately successful — attempt to open up trade with the Cantonese merchants (which accounts for the early use of the Cantonese pronunciation of the word for tea — *cha* — in English). Some time after 1644 they made their way to Amoy, which was to remain the English base for nearly a century. It was the local Amoy pronunciation of the Chinese word for tea — *t'e* —

that led to the revised word 'tea' in the English language. The East India Company was slow off the mark in bringing home supplies of the leaf, however, and it was not until 1669 that they imported their first tea into England (143½ lb. of it). The trade with China was soon well established and profitable and, after some competition in the City of London, the United East India Company was created in 1709 to amalgamate the interests of the old, original, East India Company and the recently established New or London Company.

In 1793 Britain tried to open a permanent embassy in China to help the trade. George III asked Lord Macartney to be his ambassador. He could hardly have made a better choice. George Macartney was a handsome, elegant, intelligent Irishman; a friend of Voltaire, who was a famously keen admirer of China, and with sufficient diplomatic skills to have been a successful envoy to the court of Catherine the Great of Russia when he was only 27 years old. Macartney went to China accompanied by an impressive entourage. Outside the gates of Peking the Chinese prepared a feast for the visitors. The draughtsman to the expedition, an artist named William Alexander, reported in his diary that every gentleman was given gifts and his were 'three rolls of silk, a hard lump of tea the shape and size of a bowl, a handsome china cup, an embroidered purse and a fan'. The 'lump' of tea would have been brick tea — traditionally made by steaming black or green tea and moulding it into a brick weighing about 2¼ lb., frequently embossed in the process. Macartney himself wrote in his journal on November 21st, 1793: 'In crossing into Kiangsi we passed through tea plantations and were allowed by the Viceroy to take up several teaplants in a growing state with large balls of earth adhering to them, which plants I flatter myself, I shall be able to transmit to Bengal.' His Lordship's plants failed to survive, but he also collected seeds. Sir Joseph Banks, the East India Company's botanist, who had accompanied the mission to China because of his interest in tea, was entrusted with the seeds, which under his care thrived in the botanical gardens at Calcutta. They did not, however, thrive enough to become the first tea-producing plants in India. The practical benefits of Lord Macartney's mission were negligible. English trading was to remain limited by the severe rules and restrictions in force at the port of Canton for many years.

The length of time taken by ships of the East India Company ('East Indiamen' as they were called) to complete a journey to China and back was about 4 years. They would sail from the Pool of London in a 'fleet' of three or maybe more. A ship that started loading goods for export in, say, July 1801, would be ready to sail from the Downs in January 1802, round the Cape of Good Hope by midsummer and be off the coast of China by August or September 1802. The finest China teas were picked in April and May (though further harvests followed). These teas would be ready at Canton for loading by September and the ship, with luck, could sail in January 1803. The tea could possibly be entered in London for the September sales of that year, although the March sales of 1804 were more likely. The ship would then be ready to sail again for China in January 1805.

The key officers in the trade were the 'supercargoes', who acted as chief fixers for their ships. They were renowned for their ruthless, even anarchic, business dealings, until the establishment of the monopoly of the East India Company led them to work in close association with each other. Some extracts follow, from the supercargoes' log of the voyage of the *Houghton* in 1738-9:

Feb. 22, 1738-9. Weighed in company with the *Augusta, Lynn, Prince William, Normanton, Grantham, Warwick* and *Somerset*, Indiamen. The four last came down 19th inst., and about 100 sail of other ships most of which had been wind-bound for about 2 months anchored off the South Foreland

The East Indiaman Houghton.

being calm, when the wind sprang up a S.W. Returned and anchored in the Downs. Weighed with the wind in N.B.E. in company with the Indiamen above mentioned.

Mar. 7. Anchored in Spithead, found here all our consorts but the *Augusta*, which we had lost company with in bad weather off Portland which we had got N.W. of us.

Mar. 15. Parted with the other six ships being late in the season for China, and sailing better of any of them, could lose no time.

Mar. 24. Saw the island Palma bearing S.S.W. distance 10 leagues at 8 in the morning. At noon the peak of Tenariffe bore E.B.N. and Gomera S.B.E.$\frac{1}{2}$.E.

May 24. Got soundings upon the bank 70 fathoms, greenish sand mixed with shells by which we judge Cape Lagullas to bear about N.B.E. 16 leagues. Hazy weather or we might possibly see the land.

June 30. At ten at night sounded and got ground off the island Java 90 fathoms.

[At Java a dispute arose between the supercargoes and the captain. The ship was not early but the captain evidently wanted to stop in Java to trade on his own account, a practice permitted by the Company rules. After a delay of five days only the voyage proceeded.]

July 27. At 6 o'clock in the morning weighed and stood for the River of Canton and at 4 in the afternoon anchored at Wampoa.

We have run by log from Portsmouth to this place 15,689 miles including an allowance for the Streights of Sinda and Banea and this river in 138 days having left Spithead 11th March 1738-9.

July 28th. In the evening arrived at Canton and received several visits from the merchants ...

The *Houghton* would have anchored some twelve miles downstream of Canton, where the 'factories' or warehouses of European nations lined the waterfront.

Among those to come aboard would be an officer of the 'Hoppo' or Imperial Agent to measure the ship for tax purposes; this and subsequent bureaucratic procedures provided scope for much corruption. One of the many constraints on foreign trade was the compulsion to deal only with specified Chinese merchants, later known as the 'Co-Hong', and, since little Chinese was spoken by the foreign 'devils', all dealings were conducted via Chinese interpreters who were held in low repute. At first foreigners were not allowed to remain on the mainland; later, by 1770, permanent staff were able to reside in Canton during the shipping season and retire to Macao in between. European women were never permitted in Canton. Foreigners had to contend with these restrictions until the Treaty of Nanking, which spelled out the concessions the Chinese had to make after the Opium War.

The main reason for opium was to balance trade. English markets were opening up for all kinds of oriental goods during the eighteenth and nineteenth centuries as the beginning of the Industrial Revolution and the increase of urban populations put some cash into people's pockets. There was, however, one obstacle. The Chinese, with their great skills of craftsmanship, had more goods that were desired by the West than vice versa. The Europeans wanted silk, porcelain and tea; but the Chinese wanted no European goods except bullion, and not much of that. The Dutch East

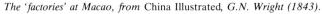

The 'factories' at Macao, from China Illustrated, *G.N. Wright (1843).*

Opium ships at Lintin, China.

India Company had at first succeeded in trading European herbs, such as sage and borage, but this did not last. By 1768 5.8 million lb. of tea was being imported into Britain alone, and during the next hundred years the trade was to double in volume at least every 25 years (mostly high-quality green tea). The solution to the unbalanced equation was to introduce something of which the British had an excess, and the Chinese badly wanted. The answer was opium, which grew abundantly in British India. The decision to create a trade in opium must be one of the worst stains on the British Imperial record; but it was wonderful for the balance of trade.

The opium trade brought home a lot of money, although it was conducted in defiance of the Chinese Imperial Authorities, and against criticism in England. Britain led the trade, but Portugal and Holland joined in and after 1815 the United States became very active. By 1832 the opium trade was reckoned to have grown to more than £5 million a year. This wealth enabled the shippers to invest in sleek, new ships, called 'opium clippers', beside which the old East Indiamen appeared inordinately slow. These clippers could make up to three return trips a year between India and China, even against the monsoon. They were beautifully fitted out, and officered by men who were more highly paid than normal.

The opium trade was symbolic of the disruption and degradation of the Chinese Empire, and led indirectly to war: the Opium War (1839-42). In 1839 a special Chinese commissioner had been sent to Canton to eradicate the opium trade and confiscate all the foreigners' supplies of opium. The British were outraged, and war broke out; unfit to combat the modern military might of the British, the Chinese were easily defeated and forced to give concessions which included Hong Kong and more trading rights for the British. It could be argued that the Chinese Imperial House had brought this disaster upon itself by resisting, from the very beginning, even the most modest establishment of regular foreign traders. The Imperial hostility had meant that the smuggling of goods, of which opium was the most profitable, became a necessity to traders if they were to balance their trade; that is, to pay for tea.

Although much tea was being consumed in Europe and America, very little was known about the drink, the plant it came from, or how it was manufactured. The names of the teas were usually English translations of Chinese names, e.g. 'Flowery Pekoe' from *pak-ho* meaning 'white hairs' or 'the down on the young buds'; 'Pekoe Souchong' from *siau-chung* meaning 'little plant'; 'Congou' from *kong-fu* meaning 'work' or 'by hand'; 'Hyson' from *yu-tsien* meaning 'before the rains'. And many of

Opium smokers.

them have been handed down to the present day. Both black and green teas were brought back; other kinds were Bohea (a black tea from a mountainous part of Fu-Kien), Orange Pekoe, Gunpowder, Bing, Caper and Twankey. Not even the different manufacture of black and green teas was known to the foreigners, until Robert Fortune managed to penetrate to the tea-growing areas in China.

Appointed collector by the Royal Horticultural Society in 1842, he soon became well acquainted with China and the Chinese; later (in 1848) he was sent to China again, specifically to collect tea plants, for the East India Company. One of the most celebrated tea-growing areas of the day was the Hwei-chow tea country, about 200 miles inland from Shanghai, and Robert Fortune determined to go there. No European had ever been allowed so far, and he had to adopt a disguise and travel in secret; because of his natural sympathy with the Chinese people, he was able to adapt to the way of life and was entertained and accepted wherever he went. He managed to collect large quantities of seed and 20,000 seedlings to send to the East India Company's Himalayan plantations (though these plants were not as successful as the indigenous Assam plants), and, though his work for them ceased after the Indian Mutiny, he continued to collect plants in China for the United States Government. He wrote a book about his Chinese travels, called *A Journey to the Tea Countries of China* (1852), and here is a condensed account of typical Chinese procedures in tea making; the scene is south-east China and the year is 1843:

... indeed, every cottager has his own little tea garden, the produce of which supplies the wants of his family, and the surplus brings him a few dollars ... In the harvest seasons are seen little family groups on the side of every hill, when the weather is dry, engaged in gathering the tea leaves. They strip the leaves off rapidly and promiscuously ... The leaves are carried home to the cottage where the operation of drying is performed. The Chinese cottages, amongst the tea hills, are simple and rude in their construction, and remind one of what we used to see in Scotland in former years, when the cow and pig lived in the same house as the peasant ... Never theless, it is in these poor cottages that a large proportion of the teas with their high-sounding names are first prepared. Barns, sheds, and other outhouses, are also frequently used for the same purpose, particularly about the temples and monasteries.

The drying pans and furnaces are of iron, round and shallow, and, in fact, are the same, or nearly the same, which the natives have in general use for cooking their rice. A row of these are built into the brick work ... the pans become hot very soon after the warm air has begun to circulate in the flue beneath them. A quantity of leaves, from a sieve or basket, are now thrown into the pans, and turned over and shaken up. The leaves are immediately affected by the heat. This part of the process lasts about five minutes, in which time the leaves lose their crispness, and become soft and pliable. They are then taken out of the pans and thrown upon a table, the upper part of which is made of split bamboo ... Three or four persons now surround the table, and the heap of tea leaves is divided into as many parcels, each individual taking as many as he can hold in his hands, and the rolling process commences. I cannot give a better idea of this operation than by comparing it to a baker working and rolling his dough ... This part of the process also lasts about five minutes, during which time a large portion of green juice has been expressed ...

When the rolling process is completed the leaves are removed from the table and shaken out for the last time ... and are exposed to the action of the air. The best days for this purpose are those which are dry and cloudy, with very little sun ... There is no stated time for this exposure, as much depends upon the nature of the weather and the convenience of the work people ... the leaves, which are now soft and pliant, are again thrown into the drying pans, and the second heating commences. Again one individual takes his post at the furnace, and keeps up a slow and steady fire. Others resume their places at the different drying pans — one at each — and commence stirring and throwing up the leaves, so that they may all have an equal share of the fire, and none get scorched or burned.

One of the reasons for Robert Fortune's trips to China was the desire of the East India Company to learn about tea in order to produce it in India. Although it took a long time to come, ultimately Indian tea was to be a deadly rival of China. The darker tea, known as 'British tea', was first auctioned in London in 1839. The U.K.'s consumption of China tea continued to rise over the next few decades, to a peak of 170 million lb. in 1886 (mainly black tea) but the future for anyone who stopped to stare at the leaves in the cup was plain to see. Indian tea rapidly increased its share of the market until by 1900 the consumption of China tea in the United Kingdom had dropped to 13 million lb., representing only 7 per cent of the total.

With their tea plantations now secure in the outposts of the Empire, the English could indulge their own xenophobic fancies. The ravings of the anti-Chinese element amongst the Indian planters are well caught in what David Crole wrote in 1897 in a textbook on tea planting:

> Let us hope, however, they will not forswear British grown teas at all events, and revert to the filthy trash that I make no doubt the 'heathen Chinee' would be only too glad to doctor up to suit the then popular taste, and palm the mixture off under some pagan name or other, to the detriment of Christian nerves and stomachs.

By 1939 the United Kingdom consumption of China tea had fallen to 1.3 million lb.; since then there has been some recovery. In 1978 Britain consumed 15 million lb. of tea from China, much of it of a rather undistinguished kind to be used in major branded blends. Specialist importers still distribute a range of fine China teas, and 'China tea' is commonly used by the public to describe scented mixtures such as Earl Grey.

4. Chanoyu: the Japanese Tea Ceremony

The first seeds of the tea plant were brought to Japan some thirty years after Lu Yu wrote his treatise in China (about A.D. 800). At first, as it had been in China, the drink was used more as a medicine than as a beverage. But the aura of good health only led the Japanese to care for tea even more enthusiastically, and in A.D. 815 the Emperor Saga issued an imperial edict commanding his people to cultivate tea and to bring large annual tributes of tea for his own household. Unfortunately, Civil Wars broke out after this, and for about two hundred years tea was forgotten. On the return of peace, however, tea cultivation was resumed. Its popularity was greatly helped by a spectacular incident involving the Mighty Minamoto Shogun Sanetomo (A.D. 1203-19). The Shogun (not unusually, one suspects) had become very ill from over-eating and summoned a Buddhist abbot, Yeisai, to help him recover. Yeisai had been responsible for re-introducing tea to Japan after the Civil War, and had written a book, *Kitcha-Yojoki* ('The Book of Tea Sanitation'), in which he claimed that tea was a sacred remedy. Faced with the irascible Shogun, the abbot naturally prescribed tea. The great general recovered, the news spread, and the reputation of tea was established as a miraculous cure.

The high regard for tea at this time is evident from the many stories of *Tocha*, a party game newly introduced from China, which centred around tea. Guests were given prizes in a tea-tasting contest to guess which tea came from the best region. *Tocha* changed gradually into the very basis of social gatherings at which tea was served. Its success shows the serious, almost ritual, attention, mixed with liveliness and fun, with which the Japanese have always treated the serving and drinking of tea. They drink mainly green tea, and the quality is very important to them. Powdered tea is still used widely in Japan, particularly for ceremonial use, when it is whisked to a foam. A cup of tea in Japan is rather a more dignified creature than the mug of 'char' in England.

The Japanese give the same attention to the cultivation of the plants, which are fed nitrates to make them very bright green. Twenty-eight days before picking the plants are shielded from the sun. The first growth gives the best quality. As the season progresses the tree gets picked further down, and in some plantations the trees end up completely bare. The newly picked leaves are steamed in a large boiler to get rid of the enzymes, and then put in a big cage and blown, so the leaves separate, and the finer ones siphoned off at the top. The leaves are dried but not roasted and emerge in bright green state. Tea picked in April is ready to be drunk in October; until then, it is kept in cool boxes.

The Japanese ascribe the beginnings of tea-drinking to the saintly Darma, a Buddhist who lived around A.D. 500. Darma dedicated seven years to a sleepless devotion to the Buddha. In order to keep awake, say the Japanese, he cut off his eyelids and threw them away. Where they fell sprouted two bushes — tea plants — whose leaves, the story suggests, would act as a stimulant for such a devoted non-sleeper. The connection between tea and Zen continued: in the late fourteenth century, the Zen priest Shuko is credited with founding the tea ceremony; the priest Sen Rikiu (1521-91) created the form in which it is practised today and his great grandson founded the Urasenke school which ever since has been headed by his direct descendants.

Throughout all the ritual the essential content of the ceremony, the principles of frugality and restraint, come from the influence of Zen Buddhism. Zen cannot be defined in words. Many Zen stories bear this out.

For example, it is related that Buddha was given a flower with a request for a statement on the proper way of life. Buddha simply held up the golden flower and gazed at it in silence. A disciple, the venerable Mahakasyapa, was transported with joy at this radiance that could not be spoken nor thought yet was transmissible from one to another.

G.B. Sansom, in his *Japan: A short cultural history* (1976), has written of the tea ceremony:

This is a subject upon which Japanese and foreign authors alike have written a great deal that is partial or exaggerated or merely foolish. There are enthusiasts who would have one believe that the Tea Masters hold the key to all problems of taste and conduct, and this is absurd, for no student of the history of this curious phenomenon can fail to see that it is a cult which lapses with dangerous ease into empty and arbitrary forms or, if it takes another turn, into mock simplicity.

This might sound like western chauvinism, but the author does later credit the tea ceremony with worthy sentiments. It can be seen as a typical example of the Japanese ability to find beauty and significance in what the West would call the trivial and the mundane.

Michael Birch is the only Englishman qualified to perform the tea ceremony as a Tea Master. He studied for many years in Japan, and now demonstrates and teaches in Britain under the auspices of the Urasenke Foundation. Here he explains the tea ceremony as it is performed today:

'The traditional tea house (*sukiya*) is specially constructed for the tea ceremony. It comprises a tea room (*cha-shitsu*), a preparation room (*mizu-ya*), a waiting room (*yoritsuki*), and a garden path (*roji*) leading to the entrance. The tea house is in a specially created wooded corner of a garden. The utensils, which are cherished as objects of art, include a tea bowl (*cha-wan*), a tea caddy (*cha-ire*), a bamboo tea whisk (*cha-sen*) and a bamboo tea scoop (*cha-shaku*). Quiet coloured clothes are preferred. On the most formal occasions plain coloured silk kimonos bearing family crests are worn together with white socks (*tabi*). The guests bring with them a small fan and small paper napkins (*kaishi*).

'The full tea ceremony consists of a first session at which a light meal is served (*kaiseki*) after which there is a short recess (*nakadachi*), then follows the principal ceremony (*goza-iri*) at which thick tea (*koicha*) is served and, finally, thin tea (*usucha*). This full ceremony occupies about four hours but a shortened version is often performed with thin tea only served and this takes an hour. At all stages respectful admiration is paid to the surroundings, the hanging scroll or flowers provided by the host, to the utensils, and to every detail of the performance.

'For the full ceremony the guests, usually five, assemble in the waiting room whence the host conducts them along the garden path, stopping for each to wash at a stone basin, to the

Michael Birch conducting a tea ceremony in London.

tea room. (Tea houses are set in gardens landscaped especially to provide the correct atmosphere.) To enter they must humble themselves by crawling through the small doorway. Inside each guest in turn admires a scroll hanging in an alcove (*tokonoma*), and in the same manner the hearth for the kettle. They take their places with the principal guest seated nearest the host. After exchanging greetings the light meal is served. This concluded, the host suggests that the guests retire to the waiting bench provided in the inner garden. By sounding a gong the host signals the guests to return. In place of the scroll there are flowers in a vase. A receptacle for fresh water and the tea caddy are in place. The host fetches the other utensils from the preparation room. The host wipes the tea caddy and scoop with a special cloth (*fukusa*), rinses the whisk in the tea bowl using hot water from the kettle, empties the tea bowl into the waste water receptacle and wipes the bowl with a piece of linen cloth (*chakin*). The host puts three scoopfuls of tea per guest into the bowl and adds a third of a ladleful of hot water from the kettle, returning the remainder to the kettle. With the whisk the mixture is whipped to the consistency of thick cream. This drink (*koicha*) is made from green tea (*matcha*) prepared from the young leaves of plants that are at least twenty years old. The bowl of tea is placed beside the hearth and the principal guest comes forward on his knees, picks up the bowl, places it on the palm of his left hand, supporting it with his right, takes one sip, praises the taste, then takes another two sips or more. He passes the bowl to the next guest after having wiped the spot from which he drank with his small paper napkin. Each guest drinks in turn in similar fashion, the last guest returning the bowl to the host. The thin tea (*usucha*) that follows, made from young green leaves from plants that are three to fifteen years old, is a foamy green mixture. The host makes the thin tea individually for each guest, who drinks the entire portion, cleans the spot from which he drank with the fingers of his right hand and then returns the bowl. When all have drunk the host carries the utensils out of the tea room, makes a silent bow to the guests, who then leave.'

Michael Birch here explains how he was trained for the ceremony.

'There are two hundred variations at least but two basic

forms of tea ceremony: the thin tea and thick tea. All the others are variations of these two types of tea—depending on the utensils and the season of the year.

'I started with just a bowl, a whisk, a small linen cloth, a tea scoop and a tea container on a tray. With the ladle there are five different movements: for pouring hot water, cold water, for hot water going on to the tea, or for hot water to wash the bowl ...

'All the arts in Japan operate within a system of franchises. They are licensed by a central school but in turn they are also licensed to issue licences. They get their income from students who do not pay much but there are so many students that it makes quite a lot. A teacher keeps some students and sends some up to the central school. I heard about this central school, the Urasenke School, and I knew that my teacher was connected with this school. She eventually arranged for me to attend on Sunday mornings. I would arrive at the class first in the hope of taking my ceremony early so that my legs would not hurt but I would usually be left until last, always kneeling, which is a sitting position with your backside between your heels — it was quite painful to do.

'One morning the Grand Master offered me a three-year scholarship, the first one to be offered to a westerner for the full-time study course. I started straight away. The actual training is in the mornings. There are lectures in the afternoon and, in the evenings, class meetings of the students about what they are going to do the next day. In Japan the teacher very seldom teaches anything because the students, in class meetings, really learn it all before ...

'The day would start at five o'clock with one group preparing the tea room and garden. There is a stone garden which has to be raked very carefully; which I found incredibly difficult to do correctly. The other gardens are moss which has to be cleaned very gently by hand. On some days this means picking out pine needles with tweezers. The pollution has got so bad in Kyoto that the moss is suffering and it is best to disturb it as little as possible.

'The tea rooms have floors consisting of one and a half inches of packed straw with a woven surface on top. First it is brushed, then wiped with a damp cloth, each morning. All the utensils for that day are taken out and cleaned. The tea containers are filled very carefully. The tea is not just put in; it

The inner and outer enclosures of a Japanese tea garden, from Landscape Gardening in Japan, *Josiah Conder (1893).*

has to be done in a certain way so it forms a small mountain shape of a certain height. It takes about twenty minutes to fill each container. The tea is sifted first. Then the fires are made up and the water put on.

'The real day starts with twenty minutes' meditation. Once a week there is a longer, one and a half hours' meditation. The students are lined up in a large, sixty mat room, each mat is six foot by three. You just sit. Not even a direction like, for instance, Yoga, where they say: clear your mind. The person who leads the meditation seems to do a lot of shouting to keep your attention in the present time. He screams and bangs his stick on the mats. He hits the students. It can be very painful or, in fact, it can be quite pleasant if you are beginning to stiffen up. You get this lovely 'thung!' — like instant massage.

'Often the session ends with the Zen Master discoursing upon a particular Buddhist expression. A great number of zen phrases express in different ways the same idea of no limitation. For example there is one scroll — *Heki so so* — just mountain after mountain going on and on for ever.

'There are three areas of learning in all Japanese arts, tea included. *Do* is the way or path (or for instance *kendo*, the way of the sword). *Gaku* is all the names and the history: where the pottery glazes originate or by whom a particular design was admired and when. Then *jitsu*, which are the actual movements. To study properly is to develop all three. In the tea ceremony the emphasis may appear to be on *jitsu* but they are hard to separate. You come to the way through the movements and the understanding and history is in all the parts.

'Zen and tea are one. There are four principles: harmony, respect, purity and tranquillity. Although the medium is Japanese together with the utensils and the mats you sit on, these four principles are no more related to national barriers than, for example, an appreciation of western music is limited to European people.'

From *The Book of Tea* by the Japanese art historian, Okakura-Kabuzo, comes an account of the last tea ceremony of the greatest Tea Master of all, the sixteenth-century Rikiu, who, under the patronage of Taiko Hideyoshi, brought the tea ceremony to a height of perfection. Hideyoshi was finally persuaded by Rikiu's enemies that the Tea Master was involved in a conspiracy to poison him. Rikiu was therefore ordered to commit suicide:

Mournfully at the appointed time the guests met at the portico. As they look into the garden path the trees seem to shudder, and in the rustling of their leaves are heard the whispers of homeless ghosts. Like solemn sentinels before the gates of Hades stand the grey stone lanterns. A wave of rare incense is wafted from the tea-room; it is the summons which bids the guests to enter. One by one they advance and take their places. In the tokonoma hangs a kakemono — a wonderful writing by an ancient monk dealing with the evanescence of all earthly things. The singing kettle, as it boils over the brazier, sounds like some cicada pouring forth his woes to departing summer. Soon the host enters the room. Each in turn is served with tea, and each in turn silently drains his cup, the host last of all. According to established etiquette, the chief guest now asks permission to examine the tea-equipage. Rikiu places the various articles before them, with the kakemono. After all have expressed admiration of their beauty, Rikiu presents one of them to each of the assembled company as a souvenir. The bowl alone he keeps. 'Never again shall this cup, polluted by the lips of misfortune, be used by man.' He speaks, and breaks the vessel into fragments.

The ceremony is over; the guests with difficulty restraining their tears, take their last farewell and leave the room. One only, the nearest and dearest, is requested to remain and witness the end. Rikiu then removes his tea-gown and carefully folds it upon the mat, thereby disclosing the immaculate white death robe which it had hitherto concealed. Tenderly he gazes on the shining blade of the fatal dagger, and in exquisite verse thus addresses it:

> Welcome to thee,
> O sword of eternity!
> Through Buddha
> And through Dharuma alike
> Thou hast cleft thy way.

With a smile upon his face Rikiu passed forth into the unknown.

Although nowadays the honour of a Tea Master would not demand death, tea and the ceremony around it still have a very strong cultural role in Japan; its influence permeates all layers of society.

5. Tea Comes to the West

Europe was ignorant of tea until an Italian, Giambattista Ramusio, edited an account of the travels of a Persian merchant, Hajji Mahomet, in a work called *Navigatione et Viaggi* (Venice, 1559). Signor Ramusio described tea as a medicine with properties similar to rhubarb (apparently, he intended this to be praise). The following year a Portuguese, Father Gaspar de Cruz, a Catholic missio-

An English coffee house, anonymous (1668).

nary in China, also mentioned it, and in 1589 a Venetian, Giovanni Botero, praised it in his treatise, *On the Causes of Greatness in Cities* (to which the modern cry of rhubarb is not far distant). In 1598 tea got its first mention in an English book, a translation of a Dutch work by Jan Hugo van Linschooten, in which he describes tea-drinking, and explains the difference between the Japanese and Chinese customs.

These effusive praises and elegant descriptions did not seem to have much impact on the English, however. The first box of leaves did not arrive in England until about 1645, via Holland, the Dutch having been the first to bring it back from China. But soon tea was being sold along with the other Dutch produce such as spices and sugar. In Holland itself it was immensely fashionable, and created enough of a social impact for the very rich to set aside special rooms for drinking it.

The first English advertisement for tea was printed in a newspaper thus:

Mercurius Politicus,

COMPRISING

The ſum of Forein Intelligence, with the Affairs now on foot in the Three Nations

O F

ENGLAND, SCOTLAND, & IRELAND.

For Information of the People.

——— *Itd vertere Seris* {Horat. de Ar. Poet.

From Thurſday *Septemb.* 23. to Thurſday *Septemb.* 30. 1658.

Advertiſements.

A Bright bay Gelding ſtoln from *Hatfeld*, in the County of *Hertford. Sept.* 23. of about 14 hand high or ſomething more, with half his Mane ſhorne and a ſtar in the Forehead, and a feather all along his Neck on the far ſide. A yong man with gray clearths of about twenty years of age, middle ſtature, went away with him. If any can give notice to the Porter at *Saliſbury houſe* in the Strand, or to the White Lion in *Hatfeld* aforeſaid, they ſhall be well rewarded for their pains.

That Excellent, and by all Phyſitians approved, *China* Drink, called by the *Chineans, Tcha*, by other Nations *Tay alias Tee*, is ſold at the *Sultaneſs-head*, a Cophee-houſe in *Sweetings* Rents by the Royal Exchange, *London*.

The English were not laggard in claiming all kinds of medicinal benefits for the new China drink. Thomas Garraway issued a broadsheet in 1657 in which he publicized the various merits of tea, which he sold at his coffee house, the Sultaness Head, in Exchange Alley in the City of London. His broadsheet included a classic puff for the medicinal properties of tea:

> When drunk moderately hot tea alleviates headaches, dropsy, scurvy, sleepiness, loss of memory, looseness of the guts, heavy dreams and colic proceeding from the wind.
>
> Taken with virgin honey instead of sugar, tea cleanes the kidneys and with milk and water it prevents consumption. If you are of corpulent body it ensures good appetite, and if you have had a surfeit it is just the thing for a gentle vomit.

Thomas Garraway's quoted prices, ranging from 16s. to 60s. per lb., are also of interest, although his claim that the previous price for tea was 120s. per lb. lacks any confirmation. It was certainly a drink for the rich.

By 1660 all fashionable society wanted to try the new drink. It excited much comment, even some poetry: Edmund Waller (1606-87) wrote:

> Venus her myrtle, Phoebus has his bays,
> Tea both excels, which she vouchsafes to praise,
> The best of Queens, the best of herbs we owe
> To that bold nation which the way did show
> To the fair region where the sun doth rise
> Whose rich productions we so justly prize,
> The muses friends, tea does our fancy aid
> Repress those vapours which the head invade
> And keep the palace of the soul serene
> Fit on her birthday to salute a Queen.

He was not only doing homage to tea, but also to his Queen, Catherine of Braganza, Charles II's wife, who was an early tea addict. Waller himself was an enthusiastic tea-drinker, especially when his pint had a couple of egg yolks beaten into it. Even Samuel Pepys tried it: 'I did send for a cup of Tee (a China drink) of which I have never drunk before.' He liked it, and ordered more.

Thomas Garraway's broadsheet suggests that already the British were drinking their tea with milk, although this was not customary in China or Japan. The reasons for this innovation are not clear; but it was certainly no fashion. In France, too, tea was taken with

Samuel Pepys, Esq., from an original by Sir Godfrey Kneller.

milk: Mme de Sévigné wrote in 1680 to a sick friend that if the milk she was advised to drink was too cold, she should take 'tea with her milk' to warm it up. Other notable French tea-drinkers of the time were Cardinal Mazarin, and Racine; but the craze for tea in France lasted only about fifty years before it was displaced by coffee and chocolate.

In England, the fame of tea was spreading more than supplies, and there was plenty of opportunity for making a quick profit. The Lords Ossory and Arlington imported some tea from Amsterdam in 1666 and sold it to their friends at a huge profit. The price of tea in Amsterdam was 3s. 4d. per lb. but they sold it in England for £2 18s. 4d.! It was not until 1681 that the East India Company gave a standing order for tea from their agents in the East; when they did, the price settled at about 12s. to 13s.

By the end of the century, the drink was well established among the rich in their fashionable coffee houses and private salons. It was so popular that it began to outrank alcohol. Taxation was levied on it, but in a curious manner: the duty was on the liquid drink, rather than the leaf, which meant that the coffee house had to make up its day's tea before the day began, so the exciseman could take his measurements. One wonders what the tea tasted like by the end of the day! Alexander Pope was a great frequenter of coffee houses, and wrote a famous couplet (supposed to be about Queen Anne at Hampton Court when she was presiding over a tea party):

> And thou great Anna, who three realms obey
> Did sometimes counsel take, and sometimes tay.

The coffee houses became such important centres of discussion that the Government feared them as centres of sedition, and Charles II tried to close them down. The outcry was such that he had to rescind his proclamation. Coffee houses continued to thrive — but were only patronized by men. The first tea shop was opened by Thomas Twining in 1717. He changed 'Tom's Coffee House' to 'The Golden Lyon' (no connection with London's famous catering firm of later years). He quickly became famous for selling tea only, and for serving both men and women.

Tea was too fashionable to avoid controversy about its merits. There were many claims of medicinal properties. Dr Jacob Bontius, a physician and naturalist of Batavia, wrote a *Historiae Naturalis* in 1642 in which he included some dialogues on tea:

ANDREAS DUREAS: You have mentioned the drink of the Chinese called *Thee*: what is your opinion thereof?
JACOB BONTIUS: The Chinese regard this drink almost as something sacred ... and they are not thought to have fulfilled the duties of hospitality till they have served you with it, just like the Mohammedons with their *caveah* [coffee]. It is of a drying quality, and banishes sleep. It is beneficial to asthmatic and wheezing patients.

Also from the East came a translation of a Chinese encomium, given in a paper by T. Povey, M.P. (October 20th, 1686);

It has, according to the Description (being translated out of the China language), these following Virtues:

1. It purifyes the Bloud of that which is grosse and Heavy.
2. It Vanquisheth havey Dreames.
3. It Easeth the brain of heavy Damps.
4. Easeth and cureth giddinesse and Paines in the Heade.
5. Prevents the Dropsie.
6. Drieth Moist humours in the Head.
7. Consumes Rawnesse.
8. Opens Obstructions.
9. Cleares the Sight.

10. Clenseth and Purifieth adult humours and a hot Liver.
11. Purifieth defects of the Bladder and Kiddneys.
12. Vanquisheth Superfluous Sleep.
13. Drives away dissines, makes one Nimble and Valinet.
14. Encourageth the heart and Drives away feare.
15. Drives away all Paines of the Collick which proceed from Wind.
16. Strengthens the Inward parts and Prevents Consumptions.
17. Strengthens the Memory.
18. Sharpens the Will and Quickens the Understanding.
19. Purgeth Safely the Gaul.
20. Strengthens the use of due benevolence.

On the Continent the Dutch continued to treat tea as a medicine, and exported it as such (they thought it was a good laxative). It seemed a good sales tactic — until the German states decided to ban all foreign medicines. Perhaps encouraged by the fanciful claims, the Germans were convinced tea was a principal cause of the shrivelled appearance of the Oriental. Its supporters were equally extreme. Doctor Waldschmidt of Marburg argued that: 'The high and mighty gentlemen who bring themselves a hundred thousand pounds of care concerning the confused situation in Europe, would do well to drink hot tea-water for the maintenance of their health.' Doctor Cornelis Decker (1648-86), who used the name 'Doctor Bontekoe', advised the drinking of 8 to 10 cups daily, and saw no harm in as many as 200, which he himself frequently consumed.

English claims were more frightening:

TEAS. Bohea [the name given to black tea from China] and Green are generally allowed to be unwholesome Herbs; if drank to excess, they hurt the Nerves (Bohea especially) and cause various distempers, as Tremors, Palseys, Vapours, Fits &c — A Gentlewoman, a great lover of Green Tea, drank it Morning and Afternoon, but was forced to leave it off, because it raked her stomach, and bred the Cholick, being (as she thought) of a feeding nature; and therefore betook herself to Alehoof or Ground-Ivy Tea. — A girl of seven years old, in my Neighbourhood, fell into the Jaundice, by drinking daily a large Quantity of Tea. — An apothecary said, if Green Tea is laid on raw liver, it will eat into it, — Drinking too much tea breeds an Asthma and Stoppage at the stomach.

'The Strode Family' by Hogarth (1697–1764).

The debate was to last a hundred years: some said tea was medicinal, others an evil herb that destroyed health. Dr Johnson (1709-84), perhaps the most famous celebrator of coffee houses, was a great advocate of tea, but Sir John Hawkins, in his *The Life of Samuel Johnson*, suggests that its effects on the great man were not entirely beneficial: 'Whenever tea appeared, he was almost raving, and his impatience to be served, his incessant calls for those ingredients which made the liquor palatable, and the haste with which he swallowed it down, he seldom failed to make that a fatigue to everyone which was intended as a general refreshment.' One of Dr Johnson's opponents in the controversy was Jonas Hanway

Dr Samuel Johnson, from an etching by P.S. Lamborn.

(1712-86), of whom Johnson with characteristic wit said: 'Hanway acquired some reputation by travelling abroad, but lost it all by travelling at home.' Hanway was a philanthropist, a traveller and an early user of the umbrella, who believed that tea was pernicious to health, obstructed industry and impoverished the nation.

Johnson proudly declared himself in the *Literary Magazine* to be: 'A hardened and shameless tea-drinker who has for many years diluted his meals with only the infusion of this fascinating plant;

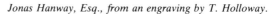

Jonas Hanway, Esq., from an engraving by T. Holloway.

A print showing a lady drinking from an early tea cup without a handle, after Nathaniel Hone.

whose kettle has scarcely time to cool, who with tea amuses the evening, with tea solaces the midnight — and with tea welcomes the morning.' In answer to Hanway's complaint that 'the very chambermaids have lost their bloom by drinking tea,' Johnson was ready with the answer: 'As for the dearth of beauty among our chambermaids: that there is less beauty in the present race of females than in those who entered the world with us, all of us are inclined to think — on whom beauty has ceased to smile!' However Johnson was a high Tory, and ready to admit that 'tea is a liquor not proper to the lower classes of the people.'

But whatever Johnson might say, the working people liked tea and were drinking it in ever increasing quantities. High taxation meant that to drink it legally was beyond the means of most people (during the eighteenth century the price was about 15s. per lb.). So smuggling flourished. Tea was brought in all round the coasts of England, and stored in caves and underground passages until redistributed by carters. Even churches were used to store the contraband. One Parson Woodford records in his diary for 1777 this incident: 'Andrews the smuggler brought me this night about 11 o'clock a bagg of Hyson Tea 6 pound weight. He frightened us a little by whistling under the parlour window just as we were going to bed. I gave him some Geneva [gin] and paid him for the tea at 10/6 per pound.' Considerably under the market price. The rewards of being caught could be grim, as one headstone witnesses:

> A little tea; one leaf I did not steal
> For guiltless bloodshed I to God appeal
> Put tea in one scale, human blood in t'other
> And think what 'tis to slay a harmless brother.

The high price of tea meant that it was often adulterated; worse, the used leaves were sometimes dried and sold again. Leaves from indigenous English trees were mixed with the tea (which was usually green anyway). Ash was a favourite 'mixer'. Richard Twining explained how it was done: the ash leaves were dried, then baked, trodden on a floor, sifted and steeped 'in copperas with sheep's dung'. Doesn't sound a delicious mixture. The first Act in England against tea adulteration was passed in 1725, but these dubious practices — both at home and abroad — continued until the Food and Drug Act of 1875. The extent of adulteration, and the diversity of the substitutes put in the tea are indicated by these new laws:

> If any dealer in tea shall dye, fabricate or manufacture any Sloe leaves, liquorice leaves, or the leaves of tea that have been used, or the leaves of any other tree, shrub or plant, in imitation of tea, or shall mix colour, stain or dye such leaves or tea with terra japonica, sugar, molasses, clay, logwood, or with any other ingredients or materials whatsoever, or shall sell, offer, or have in possession any dyes or fabricated leaves, such person shall for every pound forfeit and pay the sum of £10.

The suspect reputation of green tea made people turn to black tea.

In London the ordinary people benefited from the newly opened tea gardens in Ranelagh and Vauxhall, where tea could be drunk in exciting surroundings. Vauxhall was renowned for its lantern-lit walks, musical performances, suppers and fireworks. Ranelagh had a splendid Rotunda, with a double tier of boxes, and refreshment tables, running round inside it. It also had a delightful lake in the middle of which was an island with a Chinese house and a Venetian temple. Leopold Mozart, the composer's father, visited London in 1764 and described both gardens in a letter home:

... on entering [Ranelagh] everybody pays 2/6d. For this he may have as much bread and butter as he can eat, and as much coffee or tea as he can drink. Vauxhall is even bigger and grander. Here every person pays only one shilling for the pleasure of seeing many thousands of people, and the most beautiful lily garden, and to hear lovely music.

'A Tea Garden' by Morland (1763–1804).

The American colonies were quick to get in on the act. It had become so fashionable to drink tea that society ladies brewed pots of different varieties to suit their visitors' various tastes. But there were some disasters in the early days. News of how to make the drink was slow to arrive; so in Salem it was believed that you boiled the leaves for a long time, whereas in other towns the liquid was thrown away and the leaves were eaten! Everyone agreed that tea gardens were a grand idea (many of the early colonists were rigorously puritanical; alcohol being forbidden, tea was a good excuse for a party and some relaxation). At the end of the seventeenth century rival 'Vauxhall' and 'Ranelagh' gardens sprang up in New York. They were very well frequented, and used for breakfast as well as in the evening. Others followed: Sans Souci (the name lives on today in one of New York's top restaurants), Niblo's Garden, Contoit's, the Cherry Garden and the Tea Water Pump Garden. The Tea Water Pump of the name was attached to the spring in the garden which supplied the water for the tea. The colonists were highly conscious of the importance of water in tea, and the Corporation of New York erected a public tea-water pump whose waters were sold by carters throughout New York specifically for making tea.

In England, despite the enormous increase in popularity of the drink, its detractors did not relent. William Cobbett (1766-1835), author of *Rural Rides* and a great believer in ale as the natural drink of the Englishman, announced it was 'notorious that tea had no useful strength in it'. By simple arithmetic he demonstrated that a person may waste one month in each year preparing it and that its cost would waste a third of a labouring man's wage. That the founder of Methodism, John Wesley (1703-91), who was renowned for his firmness, could not make up his mind shows the strength of the controversy. He started by being a keen tea-drinker, but then said that tea had caused Londoners to live 'their nerves all unstrung, their bodily strength quite decayed.' And then he was seduced again, and in 1761 we hear he ordered from Josiah Wedgwood a handsome teapot, of one gallon capacity.

It was at this time that tea began its association with the temperance movement. The 'tee' in 'teetotal' may not be pure coincidence. Tea meetings, much in vogue in the eighteen thirties, had the dual benefits of attracting sinners to renounce and of raising considerable sums of money. Sometimes reformed drunkards, as star turns, served tea from huge kettles. Here is an account from *Pickwick Papers* of one of the monthly meetings of the Brick Lane

'The Breakfast Table', after Webster.

Branch of the United Grand Junction Ebenezer Temperance Association:

> The monthly meetings of the Brick Lane Branch of the United Grand Junction Ebenezer Temperance Association were held in a large room, pleasantly and airily situated at the top of a safe and commodious ladder. The president was the straight-walking Mr. Anthony Humm, a converted fireman, now a schoolmaster, and occasionally an itinerant shop-keeper, an enthusiastic and disinterested vessel, who sold tea to the members. Previous to the commencement of business the ladies sat upon forms and drank tea, till such time as they considered it expedient to leave off ...
>
> On this particular occasion the women drank tea to a most alarming extent; greatly to the horror of Mr. Weller, senior, who, utterly regardless of all Sam's admonitory nudgings, stared about him in every direction with the most undisguised astonishment.

"Sammy," whispered Mr. Weller, "if some o' these here people don't want tappin' to-morrow mornin', I ain't your father, and that's wot it is. Why, this here old lady next me is a drowndin' herself in tea."

As tea-drinking became more of a ceremony, it began to accumulate a whole range of special manners and arts. The design and manufacture of the teapot reached great heights of skill; so did the tongs, cups and saucers and the rest of the paraphernalia. For rich men, evening tea would be specially prepared and served by what were known as 'tea blenders'. The tea blenders were usually pretty girls and often came to know their employer and his friends well. Emma Hamilton, who later lived in a *ménage à trois* with her husband and Lord Nelson, originally worked as a blender. Lucky guests! King George III himself enjoyed a cup of tea, and his eldest son, the Regent, was one of the first collectors of teapots.

The tea tax rose and fell throughout the seventeenth, eighteenth and nineteenth centuries, usually increasing when the Government decided to go to war. In 1689 the system of taxing the liquid

The Boston Tea Party.

tea was replaced by a tax on the leaf, which was paid by the wholesale buyers at the East India Company's London auctions. In 1745 the duty was cut from 4s. to 1s. (although there was an additional tax of 25 per cent for any price over 4s.). This brought about a fourfold increase in sales in England, from less than 800,000 lb. in the years 1741-5 to over 2,500,000 lb. in the years 1746-50. Real consumption was still much higher than these official figures, thanks to the smugglers. As late as 1784 Pitt calculated that of the 13 million lb. of tea that were consumed in Britain, only $5\frac{1}{2}$ million had paid tax. Lower taxes decreased the incentive to smuggle, so much that even when taxes were increased again (they went up 90 per cent for the Napoleonic Wars) the smugglers never re-appeared.

Tea taxation did not only affect Britain. Parliament had the power to impose taxes on the colonies, and in times of war or economic difficulty increased them to a high level. The first Act to put a duty on tea was the 1765 Stamp Act. It was fiercely resented by the American colonists, particularly because they (and England) were at peace. They campaigned so strongly that in 1766 it was repealed. However, in 1767 Charles Townshend's rather similar Act of Trade and Revenue put the tax back on tea. Indignation was again roused, with another successful repeal — except for the tax on tea. By now the American colonists were angry and aggressive. Their slogan 'No taxation without representation' became a warcry. Determined not to drink tea from Britain, they began to import it from their old friends the Dutch. The East India Company saw their trade with America dwindling, and persuaded Parliament to pass the Tea Act of 1773, which allowed the company to trade direct from the East to America without bringing the tea back first to England and attracting duty there. The new law meant that tea became much cheaper in America, because of the saving in English duties and also the saving of freight, but 3d. of tax for Britain was still included in the price, as the colonists were well aware. Their anger continued against the home country, and tea became the symbol of revolutionary action. Ladies in many cities vowed they would drink no more tea; some cities went so far as to make the selling of tea liable to a permit; substitutes were sought, such as 'liberty tea' made from loosestrife, a wild flower.

All over America agreements were signed not to accept imports of goods from Britain, particularly tea. Some British captains, in support of the rebels, refused to take the contentious cargo across the Atlantic. But three ships finally set off for Boston with a cargo

'. . . who could blame/If Indians seized the tea,/And, chest by chest, let down the same/Into the laughing sea?' (Emerson, 1873).

of tea in the autumn of 1767. When the first ship arrived and moored in Boston harbour, however, the real trouble began. It was not allowed to discharge its cargo; but neither was it allowed to leave the harbour and return home without discharging its holds completely. The impasse was solved on December 16th, by a band of radicals, disguised as Red Indians, boarding the ship and throwing all the tea overboard. Their historic act is known as the Boston Tea Party, and other tea parties followed elsewhere. So began the American War of Independence; so, also, did the Americans stop drinking tea for some time, and turn gradually to coffee.

6. Tea and the Raj

In England, tea became the commoner's drink when the great Indian plantations began to produce their massive quantities of black tea in the nineteenth century. Ever since the time of Robert Fortune, the English had wanted to grow tea in India, but it was not until the indigenous Assam tea plants were discovered that the tea plantations became successful. The plants imported from China rarely thrived.

Although the leaves of the Assam plants had been used by the Indians as a vegetable food — eaten with oil and garlic in the Burmese fashion — and also as a drink, the trees themselves were not discovered until 1823. It was the Bruce brothers who first found them. Charles Alexander Bruce had gone out to India to serve in the East India Company. He wrote of himself:

> I left England in 1809, as midshipman, on board the H.C. ship *Windham* ... and was twice captured by the French on my way out, after two hard fought actions; was marched across the Isle of France at the end of the bayonet, and kept prisoner on board of a ship until that island was taken by the British; thus I suffered much, and twice lost all I possessed, and was never remunerated in any way. I afterwards went as an officer of a troop ship against Java, and was at the taking of that place.

In 1823 he went to Assam; his brother Robert had already started asking native chiefs about wild tea, and the result was a successful expedition which returned with the first wild tea plants from the Sadiya region. It is worth noting that the Tea Committee (which we shall meet later) was still of the opinion that black and green teas came from different plants, so different that they could be compared with bushes bearing black and red currants.

Tea cultivation in India did not begin immediately the Assam trees were found, despite enthusiasm in London for the idea. One of the main stumbling blocks was the East India Company, who feared any competition to their monopoly of China tea. In 1833, however, the Britain-China treaty expired, and the Chinese Government refused to renew it — there were even fears that all Chinese ports might be closed. The Governor-General of India, Lord William Bentinck, resolved that the East India Company should actively try to establish tea plantations in India, and appointed the first Tea Committee. The committee finally, rather grudgingly, reported that tea could indeed be grown in India, and was persuaded to begin cultivation. It made many mistakes in the early years, one of which was its persistence in using the China variety of tea, rather than the Assam, which was much better suited to local conditions. It also chose for its first site a totally unsuitable spot.

Meanwhile, Charles Bruce was working privately to reclaim from the jungle the wild areas where the plants were seen to thrive. He progressed to taking cuttings; his Chinese helpers plucked the leaf; he withered it in the sun, rolled it by hand, and dried it over charcoal fires. At last, the first tea was ready to be sent back to England. After some confusion, his methods were adopted in the Assam tea plantations. The first significant shipment of tea to London (8 chests) was delivered in 1838. The Assam Tea Company, a joint stock company, was formed in 1840, and Charles Bruce was appointed superintendent of the northern division.

The Assam Tea Company had much to learn. The countryside had been depopulated during troubles with the neighbours, and local workers were scarce. The company recruited labour in Singapore, where any oriental with a pigtail was reckoned to be qualified in all aspects of tea culture. These Chinese quarrelled endlessly on the way to Assam; some were arrested; the others refused to proceed without them; chaos ensued. Workers from other areas were decimated by cholera and the European staff suffered continually from ill health.

The Assam Company was able to trade, anyway. The Honourable East India Company could not even do that. With the breakdown of the China treaty in 1833 it was compelled to relinquish its China trade and to devote itself to government. Over the years it had acquired all the necessary powers of governing, including taxation, the right to raise armies and wage war; to mint money; and to create law and enforce it. But the price of tea was very high, and the blame for it was put squarely on to the East India Company. It found itself with no tea, and all the blame. The Indian mutiny of 1857 led to the abolition of the company the following year. India was to be directly ruled from then on by the crown. Queen Victoria's Imperial Government soon instigated more public works and trade; settlers and planters were encouraged; and large capital undertakings were financed.

In the early 1860s tea caught the imagination of all kinds of people, 'cashiered army and navy officers, medical men, engineers, veterinary surgeons, steamer captains, chemists, shop-keepers of all kinds, stable-keepers, used-up policemen, clerks and goodness knows who besides!' The Tea Rush was on! Many ill-founded enterprises were launched; mismanagement was common, and fraud was not unknown. The fever lasted surprisingly long but came to an abrupt end when widespread financial failure led to a lack of confidence in tea, and there was an equally sudden and extreme rush to get out. For a time, tea 'stank'. These financial

India before the Mutiny: the Colonel takes tea.

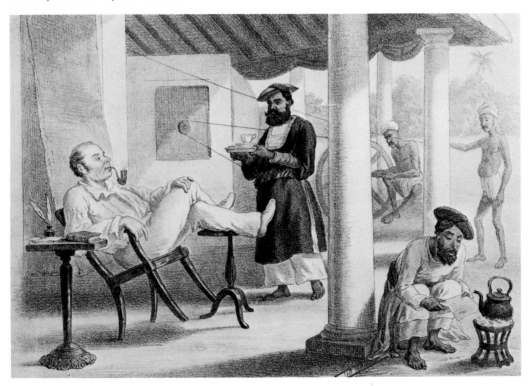

flurries had little impact on the trade's steady increase in production and export, as can be seen from the table:

	Exports
1853	366,700lb.
1859	1,205,689lb.
1865	2,758,153lb.
1866-67	6,387,988lb.
1870	13,400,000lb.

Indian tea exports, 1853-70

The business of tea planting and processing, the agency houses — and most of the drinking — was mainly European. It was not surprising, in that age of invention, that there were many attempts at mechanization. One planter, while watching his coolies hand rolling the tea leaf, conceived the idea of rolling them under an upturned table, pushed back and forth by the coolies. Putting the idea into practice, he realized that the leaves had to be held in a container. He sent to his bungalow for a pair of his white drill trousers, cut off the legs, filled them with leaf, tied up the ends and tried again. This ingenious device was the genesis of the Nelson rolling machine, which was shortly taken up by some of the productive mechanical engineering firms for which Britain was famous.

Tea exports from India rose steadily during the First World War. Indeed, it was a time of great prosperity. In 1918-19, exports amounted to 323 million lb. compared with 291 million lb. in 1913-14. The Calcutta chairman of the India Tea Association understated the case when he declared, in 1919, that the industry had come through the war without disaster!

But the immediate post-war period brought serious difficulties to the Indian planters. Prosperity had encouraged the planters to increase the number of tea bushes. It would have been a sensible policy had not the Indonesian estates managed, during the war, to capture some of the Indian planters' traditional markets, which had been starved of supplies during the war years. Russia and North America, for instance, unable to buy Indian during the war, had bought Indonesian tea, and they continued to do so. In 1919 there was an excess of Indian supply over demand. At this unfortunate moment, the U.K. Food Controller released some stocks of tea accumulated during the war. The tea market crashed. The slump was only overcome by the estates adopting higher quality plucking methods. They decided to produce less tea but to sell it at a higher price.

The appalling state of world trade after 1929 brought the competing tea-producing countries — namely India, Ceylon and the

	Rs	a	p
The clearing of 10 tracts, each 400 by 200 yards	2,000	0	0
711,110 Tea plants, at 5 annas for 300	740	11	8
Planting the above	474	0	0
Weeding each tract 3 times each year, at Rs 30 each tract	900	0	0
5 Tea houses, at Rs 50 each	250	0	0
200 hoes at one Rupee each	200	0	0
100 Axes at one Rupee each	100	0	0
100 Daws at one Rupee each	100	0	0
Dollahs, Challonis, etc., bamboo apparatus	200	0	0
8 Saws at Rs 5 each	40	0	0
Charcoal and firewood for baking the Tea	200	0	0
40 Cast-iron pans, at Rs 4 each	160	0	0
Paper for Tea boxes	100	0	0
Chalk and Indigo	50	0	0
3 Maunds of Nails of sizes, at Rs 10 per maund	30	0	0
2 Elephants at Rs 150 each	300	0	0
2 Elephant mahoots at Rs 6 each per month	144	0	0
2 Elephant mates at Rs 4 each per month	96	0	0
Rice for 2 Elephants	96	0	0
Lead for 888 boxes, at 3 seers per box containing 20 seers, at Rs 8 per maund	532	12	0
A Cooly sirdar at Rs 10 per month	120	0	0
10 Duffadars, or Overseers of coolies at Rs 3 per month	360	0	0
Coolies to collect leaves, 30 to each tract, 20 days to each crop; for 3 crops, or 60 days at Rs 3 for each man per month	1,800	0	0
4 Native carpenters, at Rs 12 ditto	576	0	0
8 Sawyers, at Rs 4 ditto	384	0	0
2 Native Lead-canister makers, at Rs 12 ditto	288	0	0
Coolies to bring in timber for Sawyers	150	0	0
5 Chinamen at Rs 30 each per month	1,800	0	0
120 Native Tea makers at Rs5 each, for 5 months, or one season	3,000	0	0
Freight to Calcutta	400	0	0
Ditto to England	1,000	0	0

				Rs	16,591	8	5
Carried over, Total outlay for 10 tracts, Co's.							

Deduct charges that are not annual, viz:-

Clearing of tracts	2,000	0	0				
Purchase of Tea plants	740	0	0				
Planting ditto	474	0	0				
Buulldng Tea houses	150	0	0				
Purchase of Hoes	200	0	0				
Do. Axes	100	0	0				
Do. Daws	100	0	0				
Do. Saws	40	0	0				
Do. Bamboo apparatus	200	0	0				
Do. Elephants	300	0	0	4,304	0	0
Total annual outlay on 10 tracts				12,287	8	5

Average product of 355,555 tea plants at 4 Sa.Wt. each plant, is 444 Mds or 17,777 Srs., or 35,554 lbs at 2s, or 1 rupee, per pound, would be   35,554 0 0

Annual profit on 10 tracts, Co's.   Rs 23,266 7 7

Annual outlay	*Co's Rs*	*Annual profits*	*Co's Rs*
For 10 tracts	12,287	On 10 tracts	23,266
For 100 tracts	1,22,870	On 100 tracts	2,32,660
For 1000 tracts	12,28,700	On 1000 tracts	23,26,600

N.B. — The deduction of Rs 4,304 not being annual outlay is not included in this calculation above 10 tracts.

Projected costings for an Indian tea plantation.

Dutch East Indies — to co-operate in an attempt to regulate the market. An International Tea Committee was set up to implement the International Tea Agreement that was signed in November

1933. The committee decided to limit production even further and to promote tea widely throughout the world.

Even though there were many problems caused by wartime conditions in north-east India during the Second World War, production during this period was higher than ever before, as can be seen by the following figures:

1939	466 million lb.
1940	474
1941	503
1942	572
1943	554
1944	509
1945	529

Indian tea production, 1939-45

Peak production was reached in 1942; later, lack of fertilizers and departure from estates of much of management and labour cut into production. These overall increases were the result of a strong market due to bulk buying by the British Government, the eclipse

Tea pluckers in Assam.

of Indonesian tea during Japanese occupation, and the difficulty of obtaining China teas. Fortuitously, the Indian plantations were ready to exploit this increased demand. During the 'thirties, the period of restriction, most poor plants had been uprooted and replaced by young, healthy, good quality plants, which had only been lightly plucked in accordance with the policy of low output and high quality. These plants were able to be plucked more heavily during the war; although some people might complain that quality had deteriorated. The slump in the 'fifties led again to a raising of quality. Direct labour costs showed a great increase during the war period. One estimate gives a fivefold increase between 1939 and the mid-'fifties; much of the increase in the wages paid was the result of the political radicalization of the late 'thirties that accompanied the rise of the Indian trade unions, the development of nationalism and, in 1947, the end of British rule and the start of independence. There were many arguments for a rise in salaries: estate workers had never been highly rewarded, although their entire families were likely to depend totally on the employment opportunities afforded by the tea estates, and during periods of slump or shortage their fortunes flickered alarmingly.

Some of these problems remain. But in many ways the story of Indian tea is one of the most successful. The marketing and publicizing of Indian tea has long out-distanced the campaign for other brands. The propaganda started in 1915, when the Cess Committee started giving gifts of tea to British army field hospitals to promote tea sales. Belgian refugees in England also benefited. But the French could not cope. The performance of instructing French troops in the preparation of a good cup of tea proved 'so beset with difficulties' that the committee gave up in despair. But the committee persevered, and their determination was rewarded when they had one of their greatest successes in India itself. Young men made their way to the houses of ladies in purdah in order to demonstrate the art of the tea table. For five days of the week the ladies were given free samples of tea; the success of the campaign was judged in terms of sales on Saturday. The outcome was that India became the world's largest consumer of tea; equally significant, perhaps, is the emphasis on quality that increasingly characterizes India's home consumption. Fierce competition from Eastern Africa, where labour is cheaper, has led the Indian market to pin its reputation on, and now to expect most success from, exporting quality teas, such as the Assams and Darjeelings.

7. Sri Lanka

This magical island, called Ceylon by the British, and now rejoicing in the title of Sri Lanka ('Lord of Lands') known to Greek and Roman as 'Taprobane', referred to as 'Serendib' in the *Arabian Nights*, lies like a teardrop off the south-east of India, and almost connected to it by coral reefs and sandbanks. The Portuguese settled there all through the sixteenth century and until the middle of the seventeenth century. They traded in exotica: apes, ivory, peacocks, jewels, gold and the valuable spices needed in the kitchens of Europe. The Dutch, who came next, added a monopoly in the cinnamon that grows wild in the jungle. When organized, this cinnamon monopoly supplied a steady 400,000 lb. annually. In 1796 the Dutch yielded possession to Britain's East India Company, who paid the British Government £60,000 a year for the cinnamon. It was coffee, not tea, that Ceylon first supplied to the West. The Dutch had acquired coffee plants by theft from Arabian sources as early as 1616 and the Netherlands East India Company had planted the seeds throughout the Dutch colonies, including Ceylon. So, two hundred years later, when the British realized that the bark of the cinnamon plants had been stripped too heavily and too often and that, anyway, substitute spices were bringing down the world price, they encouraged the Singhalese to grow alternative crops. The principal one was coffee. Until then, the Singhalese had grown coffee primarily for the flowers, which they used to decorate Buddhist shrines. The coffee mania of the mid-'thirties changed all that. Perhaps the most startling change was the upsurge of immigrants. Tamil labourers were now needed by the estates in huge quantities. The estate population was reckoned to have increased from 10,000 in 1827 to 80,000 in 1846. Much of the labour was migratory; one estimate suggests 2 million workers made the distance between the Malabar coast and the planting districts between 1837 and 1874, maybe 10 per cent of these arriving in the country to stay as permanent labour; many died on the journey.

The boom was short-lived. But, without it, the country's tea industry might never have begun. In 1869 the leaves of some coffee plants turned a dusty yellow, and the plants died. The disease, a coffee-rust fungus called *Hemileia vastatrix*, spread rapidly and brought ruin and extreme hardship to the coffee plantations. Some planters tried planting coffee in areas that were initially unaffected — particularly at higher altitudes. Indeed, during the disaster, the total acreage increased from 176,000 to as much as 275,000 acres. Another, and more successful strategy, was to diversify into other crops, and it was soon realized that tea was the plant most likely to succeed.

One of the more adventuresome planters was James Taylor, who became a notable figure in Singhalese society. Mr Taylor was born in 1835 near Laurencekirk, Kincardineshire, one of six children of a wheelwright. He came to Ceylon with a cousin in 1852 to work in the management of a successful coffee estate. He soon was managing an estate on a piece of nearby land at Loolecondra, where he remained until his death from dysentery in 1892. In the disaster of the early 1870s he decided to substitute *cinchona*, from which quinine is extracted. He obtained plants from G.H.K. Thwaites, director of the Peradeniya Royal Botanical Gardens in Ceylon. *Cinchona* was overproduced in Ceylon, however, and the price dropped. Fortunately, some three years earlier, James Taylor had already laid out a tea garden — the first proper garden in Ceylon. His pioneering efforts led the way for the development of tea throughout the island. When the author of a book* marking the centenary of the establishment of tea production in Sri Lanka enquired at Loolecondra for personal recollections of James Taylor, he was told: 'I do not remember Mr Taylor, sir, myself, but my mother and father often spoke to me about him. He was a very big man with a long beard. He weighed two hundred and forty-six pounds, and one of his fingers was as thick as this (three bunched together). That was all he needed to knock a man down ... My mother told me of his funeral. Twenty-four men carried him into Kandy, two gangs of twelve taking turns every four miles. It was about eighteen miles the way they went. They started in the morn-

100 years of Ceylon Tea, D. M. Forrest (1967)

The Dutch were the first Europeans to raise their flag in Ceylon.

ing and got to Kandy at four o'clock in the afternoon. The Singhalese woman who kept his house came out of the bungalow crying and waving her arms and would have gone with the funeral, but Mr Gordon prevented her. The Kanganis and the labourers walked behind the coffin. They called him *sami dorai* ('the master who is god').'

He was largely responsible for the energy and success of the country's tea business. He established the first of many later tea gardens, developed machinery to process the leaves, built many factories, and achieved excellent quality in the tea itself. He shunned much of the ways of the British colony. He disliked picnicking, cricket, dressing for dinner, dances, church-going and big-game hunting, and he regretted the eclipse of the more homely folk, who were the backbone of estate management, by the later arrival of the 'swells'. He maintained a wonderful flower garden, a reputation for generous hospitality in his own home, and a line of assistants who subsequently achieved fame in their own right as successful planters. Within a century of his first tea plantation the tea industry had become dominant in Sri Lanka's economy, and had, after independence, been extracted from foreign domination and transformed into a mainly Singhalese-managed national asset.

All the main requirements for tea existed or were rapidly developed. The climate was right, the soil good, and management and labour were transferred from the earlier enterprises in coffee. The Planters Association, founded in 1854, organized a voluntary tax of $2\frac{1}{2}$ per cent on exported produce which formed the basis for financing the Colombo to Kandy railway to supplement the central road system that had been mainly constructed in the eighteen fifties.

Not surprisingly, the first tea to reach London (in 1873) had been grown and plucked in Loolecondra. The dramatic growth after that is remarkable:

1873	23 lb.
1874	492
1875	1438
1876	737
1877	2105
1878	19607
1879	95969
1880	162575
1890	45,799,519
1900	149,264,603
1910	186,925,117
1920	184,770,231
1930	243,107,474
1938	235,739,000
1950	298,098,585
1960	409,783,875
1978	459,250,780

Sri Lanka tea exports, 1873-1978

The achievement of the Ceylon planters was to establish very early on and to maintain a worldwide reputation for fine quality. They chose Assam bushes, and were able to grow a lot of tea high up, which produced a good flavour. The typical Ceylon tea is black, with a small leaf and a fine, delicate flavour. The island has two monsoons, which allows continuous cropping throughout the year — while one side of the island is under the monsoon, the other is being harvested. Most of the tea estates are located in the central hill country within fifty kilometres and in a southerly direction of Kandy, the ancient capital situated at the heart of the island.

At present the oil-wealthy Middle East countries provide a good market for the higher grades of tea from Sri Lanka. They like especially the 'flowery orange pekoe' which has a good proportion of tips or buds. Thomas Lipton's Nahakettia Estate achieved a record price of over £36 per lb. for 'golden tips' tea in 1891, which was the culmination of an exaggerated concentration on achieving quality by sorting. The tips get their golden colour from juices out of the leaf when it is rolled. In fact the tips were valued more for their distinctive appearance, and the imperial splendour associated with the meticulous labour of separating them out, than for their taste. Part of the character of Ceylon tea came from the determination of each planter 'to put his own teas into his own chests and take the market by storm.' This spirited competition, fully in line with James Taylor's own philosophy, gave Ceylon tea a great impetus.

The principal basis of the British effort in Ceylon was the exploitation of the plantations in order to earn income or accumulate capital which could be remitted back home. The achievement of independence in 1948 threatened this exploitation; but recognized the value of the entrepreneurial efficiency that supported it. The plantations were seen as both an imperialist trick to be obliterated by nationalization, and as a precious national asset to be harnessed for public benefit by taxation and reform.

Part of the price of the development of the estates had been the continual annexation of village lands, and the conversion of virgin forest, so that the traditional uses of land had been interrupted. The population had also grown; some estimates say it had doubled in thirty years. The result, by the time of independence, was a recognizable land hunger, which was worsened in many respects by the presence of so many Tamil immigrants of Indian origin. Various legislation from both governments had restricted the free movement of immigrant labour; sometimes repatriating large numbers back to India, and sometimes affecting their national status, leaving many legally stateless. Since independence, although on several occasions heads of state have seemed near to agreement on the status and future of the Tamils, the problem has not been solved.

Since independence, governments have been reformist rather than radical towards the tea industry. But their intention has been clear: to ensure that the tea industry benefits its own people. The measures adopted have included severe restriction on the export of wealth, whether personal or corporate; a heavy export tax imposed on tea (the heaviest in the world); the licensing of all exports and the restriction by quota of the sales in London, thus making the Colombo auctions the largest in the world; the encouragement by government of smallholding tea production; and the restriction of opportunities for employment of foreign nationals in management

Tea pluckers in Sri Lanka.

positions. These trends reached a natural conclusion in 1974 when the tea estates were nationalized. Probably James Taylor, who never left Ceylon after his arrival in 1852 (except for a holiday in Assam devoted to the study of the tea industry) would have approved of the recent reforms that have placed the management of the tea industry back in the hands of the people of Ceylon.

8. Victorians, Edwardians and After

During the seventeenth and eighteenth centuries the fashionable hour for dinner slowly got later and later. In the seventeenth century, Pepys dined at noon; in the early eighteenth, Pope was still at table at 4.0 p.m., and by the nineteenth the gap between

The London Genuine Tea Company, 23 Ludgate Hill.

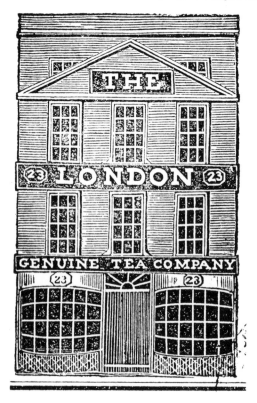

GRAND OPENING OF THE OLD HOLBORN TEA ESTABLISHMENT, 74, HIGH HOLBORN,
Took Place on Saturday, September 15th, 1849.
THE RETURNS HAVE VERY FAR EXCEEDED THE MOST EXTRAVAGANT EXPECTATIONS OF THE PROPRIETORS,
The Public having thus so generally testified their approval and determination to support us, we are fully resolved to carry out our purpose to the utmost
EFFECT A GENERAL REDUCTION ON EVERY DESCRIPTION OF TEAS AND COFFEES,
ONE FOURTH OR 25 PER CENT.

DONT PAY MORE THAN ONE SHILLING PER POUND OR THREE FARTHINGS PER OUNCE FOR COFFEE.
You can have Hawthorn's Superb Parisian Coffee at that Price, which is fully equal in aroma and strength to that sold by the Retail Grocers at 1s. 4d., 1s. 6d. & 1s. 8d., per pound.
N.B. **Our Coffees are precisely the same as the exquisite Coffees served up in the FIRST-RATE CAFES AND RESTAURANTS OF PARIS.**
DONT PAY MORE THAN 4s. PER POUND OR 3d. PER OUNCE FOR EITHER BLACK, GREEN, OR MIXED TEA.
You can have Hawthorn's Unrivalled Teas at these Prices, superior in strength and flavour to the Teas usually sold at 5s. and 5s. per pound.
N.B.--Beautiful Strong Sweetening Sugar 3½d., per pound.

Grand opening of a tea establishment.

breakfast and dinner was too large even for the most abstemious.
Reputedly it was the Duchess of Bedford who invented the meal of
tea. It began as an occasion for ladies of society to drink tea and eat
bread and butter, and later became an excuse for the most delicious and elaborate cakes and buns. By Queen Victoria's time,
'afternoon tea' was a British institution, and the drink itself had
some fanatical addicts, one of whom was the Duke of Wellington.
W.E. Gladstone was another. He boasted that between midnight
and 4.0 a.m. he drank more tea than any other member of Parliament, and when finally at home in bed, he filled his hot-water
bottle with tea for the dual purpose of keeping his toes warm and
quenching his thirst.

The need to keep the teapots full was equally urgent on both
sides of the Atlantic. The Americans' inherited taste for tea had
not been entirely quelled by the struggle for Independence and the
tea parties at Boston and elsewhere. Added to their demand for tea
was the traders' realization that they needed to bring a cargo of tea
back from China to the United States in order to fill their holds at
Canton and not return with half-empty ships. In 1784 the *Empress*

of China set off from the States via the Cape of Good Hope to China, the first American ship to do so. The mission was a great success, and there was a rush to follow it. Until 1849, ships flying the United States flag were barred from carrying cargoes direct from China to Britain. But in 1850 the competition between England and America for the tea trade began in earnest. At first, the Americans had worried the British merchants with their newly designed, fast, elegant sailing ships, called 'tea clippers', which were so much faster than the British ships. But England soon emulated the clippers, and there were many exciting races to be the first to bring back the new tea harvest. Several clippers would leave Canton on the same tide, and no more would be heard from them until they appeared in the English Channel. The races caused great excitement among both the public and the trade. Not only did the first tea home command a higher price, but prizes were awarded to the winning crew, and bets were placed on the outcome. As soon as the ships were sighted in the Downs excitement mounted. There was always a delay at the Downs while the ships waited for a favourable wind to bring them up to the port of London. Many

Refilling tea-chests at a tea warehouse.

In 1908 it was quite acceptable to drink tea out of saucers.

tea-merchants installed a wind-clock in their offices to tell them when the correct wind was blowing. Wind-clocks had large clock-faces, marked with the points of the compass, with a hand connected to a weather vane on the roof. As soon as the hand pointed to a favourable wind, if the merchant was at home, a messenger was sent off to alert him, and he would set off by horse for the docks to see the triumphant ship docking.

The greatest tea race was in 1866, when five ships set off from Foochow within twenty minutes, and reached London within two days of each other. The *Ariel* and *Taeping* came into the Thames neck and neck after ninety-nine days from Foochow. Officially the race should not have been over until the first samples had been landed, but on this occasion — to the crews' annoyance — the two owners agreed to share the 10s. a ton bonus for the first tea landed.

But races from China became old hat with the beginning of Empire tea: tea from India was auctioned first in London at the Mincing Lane sales in 1838. A tea merchant by the name of Captain Pidding bought the tea, and paid up to 34s. per lb. for it,

Twinings in the Strand in the early 1900s.

more as a gesture of solidarity with the Empire producers than as a reflection of its true value. To palates used to China teas, India teas were found to be unacceptably harsh and crude. But the China trade (as we have seen, in Chapter 3) soon collapsed, and the tea trade began to forego the search for the best 'self-drinker', which could be drunk alone, and to concentrate on a tea that could contribute a special characteristic to a blend. The Indian planters were greatly helped by the Victorian preference for all things to do with the British Empire — including India tea. Even in 1932, the tariffs gave preference to teas grown in British colonies. Fourpence was put on foreign grown tea (the target was the Netherlands East Indies tea), and 2d. on British grown.

As the Empire was disbanded, 'British' tea became less loyally supported; and anyway, the origins of the tea you bought were being obscured by the new practice of blending. The public became less aware of the different types of tea, and more aware of brand names. The growth in the number of consumer goods available since the Industrial Revolution had brought innovations in packaging and distribution, which helped increase the markets of particu-

lar brands of tea. Of the tea companies that continue to trade in
Britain today, one was there right at the beginning: Ridgways. The
great innovator was Horniman, who had introduced the idea of
selling uniform quantities of leaf in sealed, foil-lined packets, and
invented a machine for packaging. Horniman was a man of principle, interested in Parliamentary reform, and anti-slavery. His
company was eventually incorporated into J. Lyons. Ridgway, who
became insolvent as a result of the price fluctuations at the time of
the introduction of free trading in 1833, then moved from
Birmingham to London. He used advertising, and adopted the
principle of small profits and a large volume of sales to capture a
share of the market from the other established traders.

Another early company was John Cassell's. His aim in marketing tea was to turn working men away from what he called the
'demon drink' and, with his wife, he sold shilling packets in Northern industrial towns. His first publishing venture was a teetotal
news sheet printed on the press he had purchased for making the

Mr Richardson at tea, 1909.

labels for tea packets. So began the publishing firm of Cassell's, still one of the major publishing houses today.

The Vauxhall tea gardens were closed in the middle of the nineteenth century, and the public drinking of tea became impossible. But the public was soon to have an even more famous place to take tea in, to display and gossip in. A manageress of an Aerated Bread Company shop near London Bridge persuaded the firm's directors in 1864 to open up a shop to the public for tea and refreshments. It was the birth of an institution: the tea shop. The A.B.C. tea shops were followed by many more managed by Express Dairies, J. Lyons, Kardomah, Fullers and other names that excite for millions a whole way of eating, the first choice of a place to meet one's friends.

The last days of a Lyons tea shop, a mirrored and marbled palace drably disguised in peeling vinyl wallpaper, would give no idea of the glamour of its heyday, with top Hungarian orchestras and excellent tea at 2d. a cup. Tea was brought by the legendary

Nippies serving the Tommies in 1926 at Lyons Coventry Street Corner House.

British tea stall in World War I.

'nippies' (young girls who gained their name by serving their customers with the agility of youth and the expertise of professionals). The A.B.C.s and the Express Dairies fulfilled the role of providing inexpensive refreshment to the vast urban populations, especially the suburban families who come to London for shopping and a treat. Lyons Corner Houses democratized the business of eating out; their Palm Court orchestras and red plush were a treat for everyone.

During both world wars there was an increased demand for all kinds of things that could act as drugs and were socially acceptable. For many tea was an obvious choice: it was cheap and cheerful. It was, however, rationed in Britain on both occasions. In the First World War rationing was only brought in four months before Armistice, and there was never a shortage, since the Government had bought up sufficient supplies. At the beginning of the Second World War, the war stocks were dispersed by the Ministry at the docks so quickly that merchants' stocks landed up all over the country. The Ministry stepped in and sorted the tea into three grades, which it distributed to the merchants. There were plans for

British ladies attempt to convert the French to tea, 1918.

YMCA stall giving tea to 'walking wounded' at St Jean, 1917.

Field-Marshal Montgomery in the desert war.

a Government blend ('Maypole' tea) and the labels were even printed, but Lord Woolton, Minister of Food, vetoed the plan. Rationing was in force all through the war, and did not even end on Victory Day, though the weekly tea ration was increased from 2 oz. to 2½ oz. It finally ended in October 1952, and there was an immediate increase in consumption culminating in the record per capita consumption of 10 lb. in 1958.

The wartime cuppa was a great morale booster, and we are told that:

> ... no sooner did a mechanized column of British troops halt in the North African desert than, from each vehicle in the convoy, a man would come running with an empty metal drum. Into this went some sand and half a can of gasoline. A lighted match set the whole thing ablaze, the 'brew-can' was set on top, and in a few minutes every soldier was drinking his tea.

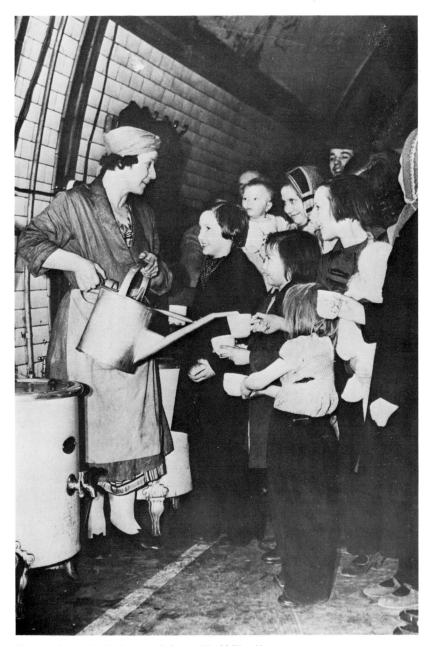

Tea supplies in the Underground during World War II.

The troops in camp drank even more. Even the persistent legend that, in order to damp their sexual ardour, N.A.A.F.I. tea was laced with bromide, did not deflect them from their right to an early morning cuppa, known as 'gunfire'.

After the boom in the 'fifties, the consumption of tea began to decline:

1956/58	9.97	1966/68	8.97
1957/59	9.88	1967/69	8.87
1958/60	9.75	68/70	8.75
1959/61	9.73	69/71	8.50
1960/62	9.70	70/72	8.40
1961/63	9.59	71/73	8.02
1962/64	9.47	72/74	7.87
1963/65	9.30	73/75	7.72
1964/66	9.09	74/76	7.83
1965/67	8.99	75/77	7.83

Three-year annual average per capita tea consumption figures for the U.K. (lb. per year)

And in 1964 the tea duty was finally — for the moment — abolished.

1660	8d. per liquid gallon
1670	2s. per liquid gallon
1689	5s. per lb. dry leaf
1700	14% of the value
1723	4s. per lb.
1745	1s. per lb.
1784	12½% of value
1796	100% of value
1836	2s. 1d. per lb.
1853	1s. 10d. per lb.
1863	1s. per lb.
1865	6d. per lb.
1890	4d. per lb.
1900	6d. per lb.
1904	8d. per lb.
1905	6d. per lb.
1906	5d. per lb.
1914	8d. per lb.
1915	1s. per lb.
1919	preferential duty of 1s. 6d. on British tea first established
1922	8d. per lb.
1924	4d. per lb.
1929	all tea duty repealed
1932	4d on foreign and 2d. on British tea
1964	abolition of tea duty

The taxation of tea in Britain

In America, there were as a matter of history more tea parties than just the one at Boston. The emotional preference there for coffee drinking had a good start and was sustained by the inclinations and habits of many later immigrants who came from Mediterranean countries with traditions of drinking coffee. But the tea chauvinists were not daunted and set out to dazzle with their East India pavilion at the Chicago Exhibition of 1893, where visitors entered through:

... a lofty gateway surmounted by four minarets ... profusely ornamented in an elaborate arabesque design ... the whole of the interior of the building was draped and decorated with carpets, rugs, silk sarees, hand-printed cloths, trophies of arms and armour, niches, and brackets supporting Indian and Burmese gods, and other figures, and the whole effect was at once rich and artistic to a degree.

The event was so successful that during the course of the exhibition the price of a cup of tea had to be raised to limit the demand.

American taste is more adapted to green tea and oolong than is British taste. Despite energetic promotion of black tea, including heavy advertising, Americans retain a more oriental approach to tea. There and on the Continent the habit of putting milk in tea has never been widely adopted, though other innovations, such as iced tea, have found great popularity.

Although tea-drinking in Britain may have declined a bit recently, it continues to thrive in Britain's ex-colonies. After Britain and Ireland, which have the highest tea consumption per head, come New Zealand, Australia and Hong Kong. In Australia the 'billy-can' is the traditional — if somewhat unsophisticated — tea container. Tea was amongst the early supplies taken to Canada by the Hudson Bay Company, and became a favourite not only amongst the trappers but also the Indians and Eskimos. They continue to warm themselves up with it in their igloos.

9. Tea Today

The popularity of tea, its forgiving nature as a plant, and the simplicity of its harvesting, have made it a rewarding crop for many Third World countries. The traditional tea-growing countries of China, India, Indonesia, Sri Lanka and Japan have been joined by many others in South America (Argentina, Brazil, Peru, Ecuador) and Africa (Kenya, Uganda, Tanzania, Malawi, Mozambique).

Tea plucking in Malawi.

Samovar in Csarist Russia.

Tea producing, which began in China and Japan, acquired some industrialization in the nineteenth century, and now has become efficiently produced in countries such as East Africa, South America and Turkey. China continues to produce a great deal of tea, and, in line with her current modernization programme, is using more and more mechanization. But she still exports the traditional high-quality teas, some of which are hand-rolled. The tea lists of the Chinese Import and Export Corporation contain over 200 named teas, which indicates that the Chinese intend to preserve their sophistication and quality in the tea market.

Indonesia is one of the most lively of the new producers. The first seeds were brought from Japan in 1825, and an early expert, J.I.L.L. Jacobson, began tea plantations as part of the Netherlands East India Company. But the Government soon abandoned the project, and it was not until 1872 that tea-growing was revived using Assam seed. In 1893 a tea officer was appointed to the Buitenzorg Botanic Gardens in Java, which have now become one of the world's leading research institutes for tea. Peak production was in 1941, when the Netherlands East Indies was the third largest tea exporter. Its black, Java tea was fine enough to compete in Russian and North American markets, causing the Indians some problems. Nowadays, the Indonesians are full of new ideas for tea, including selling it ready-made and bottled, and made into iced lollies.

Russia has traditionally been a great tea-drinking area, ever since the Empress Elizabeth received tea caravans from China in 1735, and it is still after the U.K. the largest market for India teas. During the seventeenth and eighteenth centuries, the Russians with their samovars were amongst the leading stylists of tea-drinking. They grow some black tea in Georgia, which has a sub-tropical climate so tea plants grow from May to September. The first Russian landowner to take tea seriously seems to have been Constantine Popoff, who visited China in 1899, and imported tea plants from Japan, Ceylon, the Himalayan region, Assam and

Tea-drinking ritual in Iran.

Java. Popoff was not favourable to the idea of using machinery in tea production, preferring traditional hand methods, but his ideas were not continued in Russia, and now even plucking is done by machine with a notable drop in quality. But production has increased over various five-year plans, for example from 1970 to 1975 it went from 66 thousand tonnes to 86 thousand tonnes. Most of the tea grown in the U.S.S.R. is used domestically; what is exported is either good quality tea, like that from Khrasnodar in the foothills of the Caucasus, or fannings and dust which are sold as fillers and price-reducers for blending.

Siberia and the Eastern Republics are the main consumers of brick tea and of green tea, which accounts for about one third of all tea consumed in the U.S.S.R.

Kenya is now one of the world's top exporting countries, and grows some high-quality, high-grown tea in smallholdings. Kenya now even has its own auctions, where high prices are paid for the finest teas, especially those from Kericho.

Mad hatter's tea party by Tenniel from Alice in Wonderland *by Lewis Carroll.*

English tourists on holiday in Spain.

The London tea auctions continue to dominate the international trade, however, partly because the United Kingdom consumes so much tea, and partly because financial interests in tea production in former Empire colonies remain in London. The London auctions are the only ones where the teas of the world are in competition, not merely home-grown. Nowadays, auctions are conducted on Mondays at Sir John Lyon House by the Thames in the City of London. Until 1971 they took place in a large auditorium in Plantation House, Mincing Lane. In the days of the East India Company, they were held at East India House, and the first free auction was at a dancing academy in Exchange Alley. The auctions are open to the public, and anyone — with enough money and storage space — can buy tea at them. Strangers have to give orders and limits in price to the chair or a broker. The lots contain anything from 20 to 60 chests, each weighing about 50 kilos, and they come from all over the world. Very little China tea is now auctioned, and North India teas are seasonal, so they may not appear. The difficulty in buying lots of tea at an auction is to choose a tea that can be drunk on its own, without blending. Such 'original' teas might be: Darjeeling, Uva, Dimbula, Nuwana, Eliya and some other Ceylons; an occasional Assam and perhaps, though rarely, a Nilgiri. The prices at the time of going to press average about £1.30 per kilo for a good, but common, tea; the best is about £2.80 per kilo. Bidding goes up by ½p. per kilo. Many of the large tea companies use brokers to buy their tea — partly to conceal the companies' identities, and partly to advise on quality. Brokers sometimes buy large amounts of tea and then divide it for smaller customers who wish to make a blend. All the tea warehouses used to be within a taxi ride of Mincing Lane until the Second World War, when the stocks were dispersed to prevent their destruction.

Before the tea is bought, a ritual of tea-tasting, very similar to wine-tasting, takes place. Great care is taken with the brewing of the tea samples, since they affect the price of the lot. A standard quantity of tea is put in a pot, a standard amount of boiling water added, and, after six minutes, the pots are drained into a cup, and the infused leaf is shaken into the lid of the pot, which is then placed on top of the pot. If appropriate, milk has already been put in the cup. A sample of dry leaf is also available to be inspected by the taster, who sucks a spoonful of tea into his mouth, whirls it round the taste buds at the back of the mouth, and then, like a wine-taster, spits it out. An observer of the process would judge the tasters to be highly pecuniary, since the first words they utter are a price: what they reckon the tea is worth. They then describe the tea according to the traditional terms of 'fair, bright, small leaf, brownish, well made, little mixed, brighter than ...' or perhaps 'out of condition' (O.O.C.). In an ideal world the price of tea would solely depend on these qualities of leaf, flavour, aroma and pungency, but tea is subject to weather, civil wars, and speculation.

	Date of first reported plantings	Earliest date of commercial production	Exports of tea average 1909-13	1933 standard export international tea regulation scheme	Production 1938	Production 1940	Exports 1940	Production 1950	Exports 1950	Production 1960	Exports 1960	Production 1970	Exports 1970	Production 1977	Exports 1977
TOTAL WORLD			768	809				921	867	1168,500	Excl. China 1108,600		637,500	Excl. China 1431,100	782
India	1793	1836	268	383	451	463	352	605	390	707	425	418	200	562	224
China	3254 BC		198				Export 91	76	40		91	233	30	305	68
Sri Lanka	1816	1867	189	252	247	265	246	316	298	434	409	212	208	208	185
Japan	700		40		120	128	35		15	171	21	91	1	102	3
USSR	1847	1899			19	28				83		66	36	90	
Kenya	1904	1920-25			10	12	10	15	10	30	26	41		86	70
Indonesia	1690	1825	46	174	177	181	159	77	64	101	79	44	36	64	50
Turkey	1893	1900								13		33	7	63	1
Bangladesh	circa 1860	circa 1870												37	26
Argentina										14	6	27	19	30	30
Malawi	1878	1893	.06			12	12		15	26	7	18	17	31	30
Uganda	1890				.5	1	.4	4	2	10	9	18	15	15	
Mozambique		1920-25			1	1	1			19	17	17	16	17	15
Tanzania	1920	1920-			.5	.8	.7	1	1	8		8	7	16	11
Iran	1898	1898			1	2				21	.2	19	1	24	1
Taiwan			24		27	24	19		inc. in China	38	26	27	20	26	20
Zaire						.02	.02	.5	.1		7	8	5	11	4
Brazil	1812						export .001	.2			1	5	4	7	5
Vietnam			1				5			9	4	5	1	7	3
Rwanda												1	1	5	5
Rhodesia Zimbabwe		1920-25								2	24				
Mauritius	1817	1883								1	1	3	2	4	3
Papua/New Guinea												.9	1	5	7
South Africa	1850	1877				.8	.2					.8		4	
Malaysia	1874	1874			1	1	.6	3	1	5	3	3	.9	3	.3
Cameroon											.1	1		1	
Peru										2	.04	1		3	
Equador												.3	.3	1	1
Pakistan								52	18	42	4	31	0		
Burundi												.1		1	1

Figures up to 1960 in thousand lb., then in metric tons

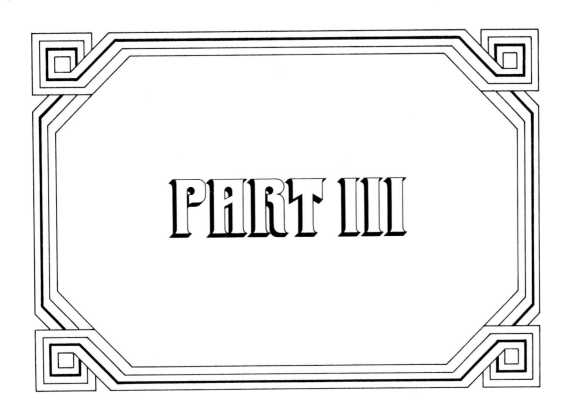

PART III

Staffordshire salt-glaze teapot, c. 1750.

10. Herbal Teas

Herbal teas (or tisanes as they are called on the Continent) have no connection with the tea plant, but are infusions of some other plant. They are called teas because they are made in the same manner, more or less, as tea — i.e. they are infusions. They are also drunk for the same purpose. Usually they are made from the leaf of a plant, dried or fresh, and sometimes the flower or root. Flavour and health benefits determine the choice of plant. Various kinds of floral, herbal and vegetable infusions have been made from time immemorial, usually to cure particular ailments. Many of them have delightful, fresh flavours, milder than those of black tea; they are usually drunk without milk, and make excellent bed-time drinks because they do not (or most of them do not) contain caffeine. The flavours may seem at first too faint for a palate used to tea and coffee, but if cultivated, the rewards are worthwhile, both in terms of the palate and the health. Blending leads to some interesting flavours, and the addition of small amounts of lemon juice or honey may bring out the flavour.

One of the advantages of herbal teas is that they are made from indigenous plants that can be gathered from the countryside, or grown in your garden. The leaves of herbal plants have their greatest flavour when freshly gathered. Few of them survive during winter, so their leaves must be dried and preserved. The best time to pick the leaves is just before the plant flowers; for it is at this time that the essential oils are present in the greatest quantities, and are concentrated in the leaves. In order to preserve the flavour, the leaves should be dried as quickly as possible but at a low temperature. They should not be exposed to the sun, but should have a current of air playing round them: hang them up in

A herb seller in Sarajevo market, Yugoslavia.

bunches, or spread them out on newspaper. When crisp, the leaves should be brushed off the stalks and stored in airtight containers.

The general rules for making a tisane are: use a jug or pot clean of the taint of ordinary tea; use boiling water; add one dessertspoonful of dried leaves for each half pint of water.

Agar Agar
Made from various seaweeds, this inhibits blood-clotting, is a remedy both for constipation and diarrhoea and has nutritive properties.

Agrimony
Infuse the entire herb: stalk, leaves and root. Culpeper recommends it for gout. It is thought to be good for purifying the blood and avoiding anaemia.

Angelica
An infusion of the leaf, taken regularly, is reckoned to cure alcoholism. It also '... drives away pestilent air.' (Gerarde's Herbal). A virtuous herb!

Balm
John Evelyn wrote of this herb that it was '... a sovereign remedy for the brain, strengthening the memory and powerfully chasing away melancholy.' Tea made from the leaves can be used as a tonic against headaches and symptoms of hysteria.

Basil
A soothing and healing herb, whose leaves are supposed to banish internal pains.

Bergamot
Taken on its own, a drink made from the leaves of bergamot is supposed to clear the head. Try mixing it with a black China tea to make a flavour like Earl Grey's tea, which is scented with bergamot oil (from the skin of the fruit).

Blackberry or bramble leaves
This infusion is a traditional remedy for diarrhoea.

Bladderwrack
The seaweed makes an infusion good for urinary disorders.

Borage
Sir Francis Bacon thought that 'The Leafe of Burrage hath an excellent spirit to repress the vapour of dusky melancholie.' For the same reason the herb was held in high esteem both by the herbalist Gerarde and the story-teller Homer.

Bourbon tea, sometimes known as Faham tea
A drink made from the orchid *Angraaecum fragrans*, which grows in the forests of Bourbon, Reunion and Mauritius.

Bran tea
Two tablespoonfuls of bran sprinkled into a pint of boiling water is simmered for twenty minutes and then strained to produce a drink that, taken last thing at night, promotes a perspiring away of colds, coughs, sore throats and voice loss. It also acts as a mild laxative.

Broom
Medieval witches used this plant for their concoctions. It is both a diuretic and a cure for jaundice. Also believed to cure 'female' afflictions.

Burdock
Use the root and seeds to make a tea which purifies the blood and cures skin diseases. Using the leaves makes a laxative.

Bushman tea
This is an infusion of the leaves of a South African tree, which is drunk as a tonic in South Africa. In Afrikaans it is known as *rooi bos*, which means 'red bush'. The beverage is supposed to possess anti-histamic properties.

Calendula
Tea made from the leaf was reputed to cure minor and major persistent skin troubles, including warts.

Camomile
The daisy-like flowers of this plant make a sleep-inducing tea; it is particularly recommended for children. Can also be used as a hair rinse.

Caragheen
Is dried seaweed; the infusion is good for disorders of the lung, throat and bowel.

Carrot
The liquor of boiled carrots purifies the blood and helps the eyesight. (The liquor of all cooked vegetables contains much of the goodness of the plants.)

Centaury
A 'sun' herb, which opens in sunlight. An infusion of the leaves is good for disorders related to the head, also for the blood, stomach and the menopause.

Chrysanthemum
Taken in regular doses a drink made from the leaves was once thought to be a cure for asthma.

Clover
Tea made from red clover flowers is an age-old remedy for tumours and swellings; also good for constipation and insomnia.

Coffee leaf
The leaves of the coffee bush can be prepared in the same way as the leaves of the tea plant, or they can be infused freshly picked. Either way, they lack the strength and aroma of coffee and the delicacy of tea.

Coltsfoot
A drink made from the leaf eases coughs and difficult breathing.

Comfrey
Use the root and leaf of this plant to make a tea for hacking coughs.

Couch grass
The tea is supposed to ease cystitis and other discomforting urinary inflammations.

Cowslip blossom
Both good for the skin and for nervous disorders, such as headaches and fits.

Dandelion
Young leaves make a drink that cleans the blood and acts also as a diuretic.

Elderflower
When separated from the stalks, the tiny white flowers of the elder tree make a fragrant drink that is equally pleasant hot or cold. It sometimes soothes the nerves or it makes a good mix with vodka or gin.

Elecampane
Tea made from the leaf has been traditionally used as a bronchial remedy.

Eucalyptus
An infusion of the leaves (from Australia) is recommended for lessening the symptoms of colds. Some Arabs flavour coffee with eucalyptus.

Faham tea (see Bourbon tea)

Fennel
Boil the seeds in water for five minutes; the pleasant aniseed-flavoured drink cleans the blood.

Ginseng
No herb has had so much claimed for it; in the second century B.C. the *Pharmacopoeia of the Heavenly Husbandman* claimed that it was: 'tonic to the five viscera, quieting the animal spirits, strengthening the soul, allaying fear, expelling evil effluvia, brightening the eyes, opening the heart, benefiting the understanding, and if taken for some time, it will invigorate the body and prolong life.' Its most famous property is perhaps aphrodisiac, but it is also used as a restorative, stimulant and to combat the effects of old age. The Chinese boil up the root (which contains the goodness) to make a tea. The root is sometimes available in the West (and has even been grown in the West), but more usually is sold as an extract which can be used neat. Teas are also available, but since they contain both leaf and flower as well as root, their power is diminished. Dosage recommended is $\frac{1}{2}$ to 1 gm. per day.

Golden rod
Gerarde said of this: 'Extolled above all other herbes for the stopping of bloud in bleeding wounds.' These properties are still recommended.

Hop
A mixture of hops and tea was once marketed in England. Hops are a general tonic, strengthening the nerves and appetite and are soporific.

Horehound
The infused leaf is said to ward off colds if taken in time, and also relieves coughs, bronchitis, etc.

Lemon balm
The infused leaf is a relaxant, and has also been used to cure the effects of old age.

Lemon grass
A fragrant tonic widely used in South Africa.

Lettuce
Use the outside leaves; as Peter Rabbit discovered, lettuce is very soporific.

Limeflower
A refreshing drink taken hot or cold; it eases a headache and induces peaceful sleep.

Linseed
To ease a 'tight' or sore chest, make an infusion using the crushed, rather than the whole, seeds.

Lobelia
Contains lobeline, similar to nicotine. The infused leaves act as sedative and tranquillizer. Orthodox medicine uses the plant for bronchial disorders.

Marjoram
Wild marjoram is origano, of which Gerarde said: 'Oragany is very good against the wambling of the stomach, and stayeth the desire to vomit, especially at sea. It may be used to good purpose by such as cannot brook their meat.' Tea made from the leaf.

Marshmallow
An infusion of the leaves of this plant will ease pain caused by internal inflammation

Maté, also known as Yerba maté or Paraguay tea
Among the gains of the Spanish conquest were the lessons in the pharmacology of rare South American plants that the Jesuits had from the Indians. Notable examples were *cinchona* from which quinine is derived and the infusion known as maté, yerba or Paraguay tea from a type of holly tree, *Ilex paraguayensis*. The tree is not very large, has a smooth whitish bark and its boughs and dark glossy leaves resemble the laurel. The flowers are small and white growing in clusters. The fruit is in the form of red berries resembling Christmas holly. The leaves are plucked and dried, fired (scorched) and pounded into a powder. The pulverized leaf is left in sacks until dry; sometimes it is dried in raw hides.

An infusion with boiling water is made in the normal way which was customarily done in a calabash or maté, often silver mounted, with sugar, milk or lemon added to the leaves (yerba). The beverage was then taken, very hot, through a metal (usually silver) or reed tube, called a 'bombilla', with a strainer at one end. Nowadays mundane teapots, cups and saucers are usually used.

Maté contains caffeine and therefore acts as a restorative much as tea does. Its rather leafy taste is not difficult to appreciate.

Meadow sweet
Gerarde said of this herb: 'The smell therefore makes the hart merrie, delighteth the senses.' A diuretic, good for fevers and blood pressure.

Mistletoe
An infusion of the leaves is reputed to cure 'female' disorders. The plant was worshipped by the Druids; berries are poisonous but can be used in small doses for nervous disorders.

Moss
The variety known as Irish moss is recommended for sufferers from bronchial illnesses. Wash the moss thoroughly and leave it to soak in cold water for ten minutes before using it.

Mullein
The infusion cures ailments of the lung.

Nettle
This plant was sacred to the Saxons. The leaves make a drink rich in iron, which is recommended for colds. They must be harvested before June. The liquor from boiled nettle seeds was an old remedy for consumption.

Orchid (see Bourbon)

Parsley
Another drink containing iron, this one recommended for disorders of the bladder and kidneys.

Pennyroyal
The leaf, when infused, is good for removing headaches. It should not be taken when pregnant.

Peppermint
Infused leaves principally aid indigestion; also colds.

Psyllium seed
Good for the bowels, as it absorbs water from the gut.

Raspberry leaf
To alleviate menstrual pains.

Rice tea
This was once quite a common drink in those nurseries of England where tea was banned as being too strong. Roast the rice slowly in the oven until it is well browned. Make an infusion as for ordinary tea but allow it to stand for half an hour before drinking. Rice is already mixed with some Japanese tea.

Rosehip
A favourite, delicate tisane.

Rosemary
An infusion of the leaf is said to stimulate the memory.

Rue
Tea made from the leaf is reputed to cure a wide range of ailments of eyesight, veins, arteries, high blood pressure, cramp, painful menstruation, and menopause. Not to be taken when pregnant or in large quantities.

Sage
Infused leaf brings back a lost voice or eases sore throats.

Skullcap
Acts as a sedative and cure for headaches.

Strawberry
The fruit acts as a laxative but the leaves made into a drink used to be given to children to stop bed-wetting.

Sunflower seeds
Boil the seeds and simmer for twenty minutes. Use the liquor as a cough medicine.

Thyme
Tea made from the leaf alleviates sore throats, mild coughs and shortness of breath.

Valerian
This is one of the most powerful and useful of herbal remedies. Hitler was said to be 'on it'. The infusion acts as a tranquillizer and sedative and is used to cure hysteria and anxiety symptoms.

Violets
Culpeper found that 'The flowers ease pains in the head caused by want of sleep.'

Yarrow
The infusion is supposed to relieve colds and flu.

Youpan
A type of holly tree, the *Ilex cassine*, provides the leaves from which certain North American Indians made a tea-like infusion.

Here are a few suggested blends of herbs for infusing; there are no rules, you can try thousands of permutations:

Balm tea (from a nineteenth-century recipe book)
12 sprigs balm, 6 cloves, the juice of half a lemon and a pint of boiling water are left to infuse for one hour. The liquor tastes like acid drops and should be taken at night by people with colds. (Similar recipes often call for the addition of half a dozen sprigs of nettle.)

Herb tea (a seventeenth-century substitute for tea)
Mix five ounces of rose leaves, one of rosemary and two of balm. Use dried leaves chopped small and mixed well.

Sage tea (from The New Art of Cookery *by Richard Briggs, 1788)*
'Take a little sage, a little Balm, put it into a pan, slice a lemon peel and all, a few knobs of sugar, one glass of white wine; pour on these two or three quarts of boiling water; cover it, and drink when thirsty. When you think it strong enough of the herbs take them out otherwise it will make it bitter.'

Herb tea (from a dictionary of cookery, 1820)
'The following proportions are recommended by a well known herbalist: Agrimony, balm, tormentil, wild marjoram of each one ounce; red roses, cowslip flowers, blackcurrant leaves of each a quarter of an ounce. Cut small and mix. A heaped tablespoonful is

enough for two persons, made as China tea, with sugar and cream, or milk if approved. The following substitute for tea is also recommended:- Hawthorn leaves dried, ten parts; sage and balm, one part. Mix well together, and use as above.'

Linseed tea
1 oz. linseed, ½ oz. liquorice, a strip of lemon rind, 1 quart of water, ½ oz. barley sugar, ½ oz. brown sugar.
   Boil the linseed and lemon peel in the water and allow them to simmer for half an hour before adding the other ingredients; when these have dissolved the tea is ready for use.

Herb tea with linseed
Equal parts of aniseed, fennel, caraway and coriander; a dessertspoonful of the mixture with each half pint of boiling water will make a drink that is good hot or cold.

Herb tea
Use one handful each of borage, sorrel, endive, cinque foil, add two or three handfuls of barley and half a handful of red fennel roots together with small amounts of liquorice, honey, figs, dates and raisins. Boil all these in one gallon of water until it is reduced to about three pints. Strain the liquor off and bottle it.

Elderflower tea
1 part of dried elderflowers added to 3 of standard Indian tea converts it into something very like Darjeeling; or the elderflowers in a muslin bag may be stored with the tea.

This list may have been a help to get you started. Part of the appeal of herbal teas and surrogates is their lack of commercialization; a few attractive, old-established herb merchants still exist, such as Culpepers, but otherwise you must search for your own ingredients. On the Continent, tisanes are more readily available; they are sold in supermarkets, and a lot of the old herbal shops still exist. Cafés also are more likely to serve tisanes.

11. Tea Cookery

We tend to make tea unimaginatively with milk or lemon, but there are other ways of making it:

Bitter tea, from Cashmere
Black tea is boiled, and to it is added aniseed and salt.

Cream tea, from Turkestan
Black tea is boiled, taken off the heat and cream is added. Pieces of bread are soaked in it and eaten for breakfast.

Cinnamon tea, from Sri Lanka
Instead of putting milk in the tea stir it with a stick of cinnamon. This is a good drink for the winter.

Mint tea
Fresh or dried mint is infused with the tea, usually green, in many parts of North Africa.

Russian tea
Pour the hot tea on to slices of lemon or on to a teaspoonful of jam.

An Indian tea
A tea is made in India, and in African countries where Indians live, by boiling milk and tea, with or without some additional water and sugar, and adding the flavouring of an aromatic spice.

Cold tea (from Dictionary of Cookery, *1820)*
'The value of cold tea as a beverage is not sufficiently known.

Literary men and others accustomed to a sedentary occupation would find one or two cups of cold tea taken without either milk or sugar to be as stimulating as the same quantity of sherry, whilst there would be no fear of the drowsiness or diminution of the working power which might arise from imbibing either wine or spirit. The taste of cold tea is an easily acquired one, and worth cultivating by those who require an occasional and harmless stimulant.'

Iced tea
It is best to use a non-astringent tea, such as Ceylon or Keemun.
1) Cover, cool and strain tea and put it to chill.
   Or;
2) Put tea leaves into cold water and leave overnight, strain the liquor off next morning.
To iced tea can be added cucumber, mint, orange, lemon or other fruits.

Tea can be used to make other drinks:

Fruit and mint tea punch
1 pint of hot tea, up to 6 oz. sugar, $\frac{1}{2}$ pint orange juice, $\frac{1}{4}$ pint lemon juice, sliced orange, lemon, strawberries or other fruits, ice cubes and mint leaves.
   Strain the hot tea onto the sugar, add the citrus juices. When the liquor is cold add it to the fruit, ice and mint.

Hot spiced honey punch
2 tablespoons lemon juice, up to 4 tablespoonfuls honey, 3 cloves, pinch of nutmeg, a pinch of ginger and a 2 inch piece of cinnamon are all infused with 3 pints of hot tea for 10 minutes. Strain and reheat to serve with slices of lemon and a few cloves.

It can also be used in savoury dishes and as a flavouring for ices and sorbets:

Cheese fondue
$1\frac{1}{2}$ level tablespoons cornflour, 2 tablespoons dry sherry, 1 clove garlic, $\frac{1}{2}$ pint tea, 1 lb. Cheddar cheese (grated), a medium size French loaf.
   Mix the cornflour to a smooth paste with the sherry. Crush the garlic into a flameproof casserole and rub it around. Put the

casserole on to heat, add the tea and bring to the boil. Add the cheese a handful at a time, stir until melted. Add cornflour mixture. Bring to boil stirring continuously. Season to taste with salt and pepper, simmer for 2 minutes. Stand on plate warmer or spirit lamp. Fondue is traditionally eaten by dipping cubes of bread on the end of a fork in to the mixture while it is being kept very hot.

Country tea bread
7 oz. mixed currants, sultanas and seedless raisins, 1 oz. chopped peel, $\frac{1}{4}$ pint tea, 4 oz. clear honey, 1 egg (beaten), 8 oz. self-raising flour, 1 oz. melted butter, salt, $\frac{1}{4}$ oz. chopped walnuts, $\frac{1}{4}$ oz. demerara sugar.

Put the fruit, peel, tea and all but one teaspoonful of the honey in to a bowl, cover and leave overnight. The next day stir in the beaten egg, sifted flour, salt and melted butter, in that order. Put the mixture in to a greased 1 lb. bread tin and bake for about 70 minutes at 350°F. mark 4. After 50 minutes cooking remove the loaf from the oven, brush the top with honey sprinkle it with nuts and sugar, trickle more honey over and return to the oven to finish cooking.

Pork, liver and tea pâté (a recipe from The Tea Council)
1 oz. butter, 2 onions, roughly chopped, $\frac{1}{2}$ pint freshly made tea, 1 lb. pigs liver, sliced, $\frac{1}{2}$ lb. boned belly of pork, cubed, $\frac{1}{2}$ lb. boned blade bone of pork, cubed, salt and pepper, 2 bayleaves, 2 good pinches dried thyme, 2-3 cloves garlic crushed, 4 strips lemon rind, 1 egg, 2 level teaspoons concentrated tomato purée, 1 teaspoon Worcester sauce, $\frac{1}{4}$ oz. powdered gelatine, 2 tablespoons brandy.

Melt butter and fry onions slowly until soft but not coloured. Add tea, liver, pork, seasoning, herbs, garlic, lemon rind and bones from the meat. Bring to the boil and simmer for $1\frac{1}{4}$ hours. Pour through a sieve retaining the liquid. Discard bay leaves, lemon rind and bones.

Chop about $\frac{1}{2}$ the liver and mince rest with pork and onions using fine plate. Mix together and add egg, purée, sauce and $\frac{1}{4}$ pint meat liquid beaten together. Transfer to a greased dish or tin $8\frac{1}{2}''$ x $3\frac{1}{2}''$ approximately and bake for 45 minutes at 325°F. mark 3.

Leave in dish and pour in gelatine dissolved in 1/8 pint meat liquid with brandy added. Leave until liquid is absorbed. Cover with paper. Put in refrigerator for several hours and turn out and garnish.

Tea cream (from The Cooks Dictionary and Household Directory *by Richard Dolby, 1833)*
Infuse an ounce of the best green tea in half a pint of boiling milk, simmer it five minutes, then strain it through a tammy [sieve], pressing the leaves well. Boil a pint of rich cream, add to it the yolks of four eggs, well beaten, and a sufficient quantity of clarified sugar; pour this whilst hot to the milk, stir them together well; put in as much clarified isinglass* as will set it, and pour the cream into the mould or glasses; place them on ice; when perfectly cold, turn it out of the mould, or serve in the glasses.

Tea cream (as above)
Boil two drachms† (or more) of good green tea in a quart of milk; in a few minutes strain it; add three yolks of eggs well beaten, a quarter of a pound of powdered sugar; set it on the fire, and reduce it to half, then strain it again; when cold, serve it.

Tea Sorbet
¾ oz. tea, ½ pint of boiling water, 6 oz. caster sugar, juice of two lemons, one egg white. Sprigs of mint or borage as decoration.
   Pour the water, freshly boiled, on the tea and leave to infuse for five minutes. Strain on to the sugar and lemon juice and stir well. Allow the mixture to cool and then put it into a freezer. When half frozen fold into it the egg white beaten very stiffly. Serve the sorbet, still a little soft, with a decoration of mint or borage leaves in the summer or slivers of lemon in the winter.

Tea Ice Cream
1 pint of milk, 1″ vanilla pod, 2 level tablespoonfuls of dry tea, 4 eggs, 6 oz. caster sugar, ½ pint of double cream.
   Bring the milk, with the vanilla in it, to the boil, pour this over the tea and allow to brew for five minutes, then strain off the liquor. Beat the eggs and add the caster sugar, continue beating until the mixture is perfectly smooth. Stir in the prepared tea liquor. Put this mixture in a bowl above boiling water and stir until the mixture thickens. Pour into a basin and allow to cool. Whip the cream until it peaks and fold into the cool mixture. Freeze.

---

*You can substitute cornflour.

†1 drachm = 1/8 oz.

Tea Jelly I

Two lemons, one packet of lemon flavoured jelly, $\frac{3}{4}$ pint of strong, freshly brewed tea, cream to decorate.

Grate the skins of the lemons. Put the jelly into a measure and make up to one pint with the hot tea. Stir until dissolved. Add the lemon peel and pour into a mould or moulds. Allow to cool.

Tea jelly II

$\frac{1}{2}$ pint evaporated milk, 2 yolks of egg, 4 oz. sugar, $\frac{3}{4}$ oz. gelatine, $\frac{1}{2}$ pint strong cold tea.

Whisk egg yolks and add the sugar, gradually add half the milk and all the tea. Put the mixture into a double saucepan, whisk it over the boiling water until it thickens, add the gelatine, dissolved in a little warm water. Whip the remainder of the milk and fold this into the cooling mixture. Pour into a rinsed mould and put on ice to set.

Tea cream

1 oz. good tea, $\frac{3}{4}$ oz. of gelatine, $\frac{1}{2}$ pint milk, $\frac{1}{2}$ pint cream, sugar to taste.

Bring the milk to boiling point, pour over the tea, leave to infuse for 20 minutes, strain and add half the cream. Dissolve the gelatine in a little boiling water, strain it into the mixture, sweeten to taste, leave to cool. Whip the remainder of the cream until stiff, fold into the mixture, pour into a mould, rinsed with cold water, to set.

After the liquid has been drunk, the leaves still have a lot of uses:

Shamma, from Turkestan

The used leaves are chewed after meals in much the same way as betel is chewed in India. Chewing the leaves helps to allay fatigue on a journey when food is scarce.

Used tea leaves are excellent for the compost heap, and as food for roses.

The cold liquor makes an eye wash, skin lotion or hair rinse. The weakly acidic nature provides some buffering action and the oxidized polyphenols act as bacteriocides.

Cold or lukewarm tea is ideal for finger bowls, after the Chinese practice.

From the days of adulterated tea — a test (from Mrs Beeton):
Drop a pinch in the fire; the bluer the flame the better the tea.

Tea stains on linen
'If fine linen is stained with tea, even after a long time, the stains can be removed by steeping in borax and water.'

The Best Way is a book of household hints and recipes which claimed to be the 'cheapest cookery book in the world' and cost 6d. in 1916. It gives some hints for the use of cold tea:

> Save spent leaves for a few days, then steep them in a tin pail or pan for half an hour; strain through a sieve and use the tea to clean varnished wood. It requires very little elbow polish, as the tea acts as a strong detergent, cleansing the paint from all impurities, and making it equal to new. It cleanses window sashes and oilcloths; indeed any varnished surface is improved by its application. It washes window panes and mirrors much better than water, and is excellent for cleaning black walnut and looking-glass frames. It will not do to wash unvarnished paints with it.

The scientific journal, *Nature*, of August 15th, 1942, reported an experiment in which rabbits were fed on a diet containing spent tea leaves. The protein content is indigestible because of the high tannin content. The leaves are only suitable as a substitute for some of the bran ration. It cut down the rabbits appetite for water.

Tea Pillow
A hint from China: a pillow stuffed with tea leaves for the bed is good for the eyes.

Tea Leaves, Their use (from a pre war book of cookery and household management)
'Never throw away tea leaves. When cleaning your teapot squeeze the leaves very dry, throw them into a jar, and mix them with a little coarse kitchen salt. When turning out a room that has a thick carpet on the floor, before you start brushing your carpet, sprinkle the mixture over it, well in the corners, as it gathers up all dust. If you pour boiling water on used leaves and leave for an hour in a bottle, the liquid can be used to clean mirrors, glasses, varnished doors, furniture, linoleum and muddy black suede shoes, also black and navy blue skirts.'

As for what to eat at tea-time, the range is enormous, but the traditional accompaniments of a cup of tea are:

Afternoon tea scones (from Mrs Beeton*)
4 oz. flour, 1 oz. butter, 1 tablespoonful of caster sugar, $\frac{1}{2}$ teaspoonful bicarbonate of soda, 1 egg, a little cold water (the egg may be omitted).

Rub the butter lightly into the flour and add the remaining dry ingredients. Beat and stir in the egg, adding cold water or milk to make a light dough. Roll out thin, cut into small rounds, and bake on a hot griddle or in a sharp oven. Present-day oven setting would be 379°F., gas mark 5. Time: about 10 minutes to bake. Sufficient for 8 scones.

Tea Kisses
These are *petit four* meringue biscuits.
2 egg whites, 4 oz. sugar, grated rind of $\frac{1}{2}$ lemon.

Beat the egg whites very stiff. Add sugar and the lemon rind gradually, continue beating until the mixture is very stiff. Drop the mixture from the end of a spoon or out of an icing syringe on to an oiled baking tray. Bake 50 minutes at 250°F., mark $\frac{1}{4}$.

Madeleines
These fragile cakes baked in small scallop-shaped tins are the speciality of Commercy in France. It was while drinking tea and eating madeleines that Proust started on his long-remembered journey to past times.
2 large eggs, up to 6 oz. softened butter, $\frac{1}{2}$ tablespoon lemon juice, 6 oz. plain flour.

Beat the softened butter until it has the consistency of thick cream. Whip together the eggs, sugar and lemon juice until the volume has nearly doubled and the mixture looks pale and fluffy, gradually stir in the flour and then the butter, mix all the ingredients thoroughly before baking in the middle of a preheated 350°F., mark 4 oven for about half an hour.

Tea cakes (from Mrs Beeton)
2 lb. flour, $\frac{1}{2}$ teaspoon salt, $\frac{1}{4}$ lb. butter, margarine or lard, 1 egg, $\frac{1}{2}$ oz. yeast, warm milk.

Put the flour into a baron [large mixing bowl], mix with it the salt, and rub in the fat, make a bay [hollow], pour in the warm yeast

* *Mrs Beeton's Book of Household Management*, 1861.

dissolved in a little warm milk, add the egg, and then sufficient warm milk to make the whole into a smooth paste, and knead it well. Let it rise near the fire, and when well risen form it into cakes; place them on tins, let them rise again before placing them in the oven, and bake from $\frac{1}{4}$ to $\frac{1}{2}$ an hour in a moderate oven.

These cakes are also very nice with the addition of a few currants and a little sugar to the other ingredients, which should be put in after the paste is moistened.

The cakes should be buttered and eaten hot as soon as baked; but when stale they are very nice split and toasted; or, if dipped in milk or even water, and covered with a basin and placed in the oven till hot, they will be almost equal to new.

Sufficient to make 8 tea cakes.

Tea cake toast (from Mrs Beeton)
Cut each tea cake into 3 or 4 slices according to its thickness; toast them on both sides before a nice clear fire, and as each slice is done, spread it with butter on both sides. When a cake is toasted, pile the slices one on top of the other, cut them into quarters, put them on a very hot plate and send the cakes immediately to table. As they are wanted send them in hot, 1 or 2 at a time, for they spoil if allowed to stand, unless kept over boiling water.

12. Teaware

During the T'ang dynasty (A.D. 620-904) the Chinese people were becoming the world's first tea drinkers. It was also during this same period that a pottery was perfected superior to any seen before. It is translucent, hard and glazed: known as 'china' by the English. It was the Dutch and Portuguese traders who brought the first Chinese pottery to Europe and much of what they brought was for use as tea equipment. Those pots most commonly imported were small, red-brown pots of stone ware, not porcelain, made near Soochow and given the Portuguese name *boccarro* (*bocca* = mouth) because they are large mouthed. Most of these early pots

Cups without handles in the eighteenth century followed the Chinese style of drinking tea out of bowls.

Chelsea porcelain teapot, c. 1752–6.

that were used for tea were not actually teapots at all, but wine
pots. The Chinese and Japanese prepare the drink by pouring the
boiling water onto tea leaves in the small bowls from which they
subsequently drink. It was these bowls that became tea cups in
Europe. In the first half of the eighteenth century the Chinese
added handles and saucers to the bowls that they were then making
for the export trade.

With typical reticence, the Chinese would not reveal the secret
of porcelain, and so in Europe potters could only imitate, using
tin-glazed, decorated earthenware known as 'faience'. Delft ware
was a seventeenth-century Dutch copy of Chinese blue-and-white
porcelain in faience, and this in turn was copied in England with
blue transfers. It was not until 1709 that two Germans, Johann
Friedrich Böttger and Ehrenfried Walter von Tschirnhausen,
found the answer to the riddle of porcelain: kaolin clay. They set
up the Meissen pottery near Dresden, which began producing the
first European porcelain of quality comparable with Chinese.

Derby porcelain teapot, c. *1756–60.*

Leeds creamware teapot, c. *1775.*

Worcester tea canisters and teapot, 1770–80.

Another Chinese legacy was the tradition of using mythological symbols as shapes for their utensils; in the West this was debased into teapots looking like Chinamen, and the thatched cottages of today. When the East India Company began bringing back Chinese pottery, a vogue for Chinoiserie came to Britain.

In the eighteenth century, British craftsmen began to enter the field of teaware; Staffordshire factories soon were making teapots in all shapes and sizes, in a great variety of styles, from salt-glazed stoneware, which was intended to imitate porcelain. This tradition in Staffordshire was the starting point for Josiah Wedgwood's successful harnessing of design and craftsmanship to the modern industrial production unit. Wedgwood took great pains to ensure that his products, and in particular teapots, were flawless in every detail. His wife tested each development in their own home. Wedgwood's most important product is now regarded as his cream-ware or 'Queens-ware', (called after Queen Charlotte), which is a fine white earthenware still widely used. His more spectacular product, which gained such fame that it was copied on the Continent, was 'jasper' ware, often blue adorned with white cameo reliefs — many of them designed by Flaxman.

English porcelain, which developed side by side with salt glaze and Wedgwood ware, was known as 'soft-paste' porcelain, as distinct from the hard-paste porcelain of China and Germany. Using this material, also adopted by the French at Sèvres, the potters of Chelsea, Bow, Worcester and Derby were able to pro-

Silver teapot, 1830.

duce porcelain tea services which were greatly sought after. A formula for porcelain was developed by Josiah Spode II in the nineteenth century known as bone china; it achieved a world market through the products of Rockingham, Coalport, Copeland, Swansea, Derby, Worcester and, of course, Spode.

It is interesting to see how the size and shape of teapots have altered over the years: shape has followed fashion in taste, so that the eighteenth-century were rococo, the late eighteenth-century were neo-classical, and the Victorian were heavily ornamented. The size of teapots has reflected the price of tea; when in the seventeenth century, tea was 3 guineas per lb., pots were precious and tiny. When tea became cheaper, pots were much larger, and made of more mundane material. The tea service developed in the eighteenth century, when tea was still expensive, and teapots continued to be on the small side. A full tea service consisted of: a teapot and cover, a coffee pot and cover, sugar bowl, stand and cover, 12 tea bowls or cups and saucers, 6 coffee cups, milk jug and cover, slop bowl, spoon tray, teapot stand and tea canister. Later came large plates for bread and butter, and in mid-Victorian times little plates. The canister containing the tea was taken to the table,

Each to his taste: (above) *a tank teapot, 1951;* (below) *tea set, 1935.*

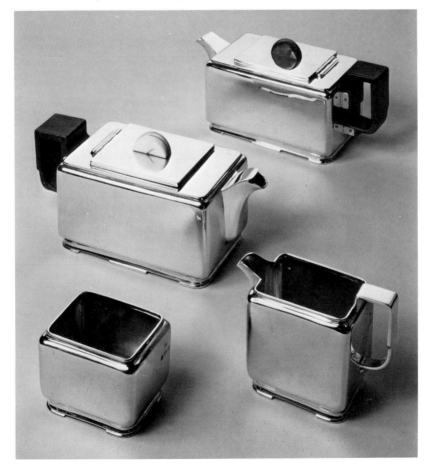

as tea was made on the spot, and so canisters were decorated. Sometimes there would be two canisters, one for green and one for black tea, and the teas would be mixed in the pot. Or pure teas might be kept in canisters: some of them are marked 'Bohea' or 'Hyson'. The canisters were yet another inheritance from the East — the Chinese and Japanese had very fine, ornamented tea jars, made of porcelain. When the price of tea was high, canisters were made by gifted craftsmen, in silver, but as the price of tea dropped they degenerated to lead-lined wooden boxes and finally metal caddies, relegated to the kitchen.

The traditional kettle — or cauldron — was discovered to be impractical for pouring boiling water over tea leaves. A Chinese shaped pot was adopted, with its spout and top handle.

One wonders what future generations will be able to marvel over when they consider the mid-twentieth century mug and teabag.

13. How to Read the Leaves

Fortune has made tea and tea has made fortunes, no surprise then that the leaves reveal fortunes:

grasp the cup by the handle in the left hand

swirl the dregs three times counter-clockwise

gently invert the cup in the saucer

turn it the right way up again

inspect the bottom of the cup and the shape the tea leaves make there

use the list below to reinforce your powers of interpretation

note: avoid teabags; in the Southern hemisphere it would be worth trying a clockwise swirl using the right hand.

anchor — voyage
cat — treachery
cow — prosperity
dog — good friends
book — revelations
clouds — doubts, problems
cross — suffering
egg — increase in luck
flowers — love, honour, esteem
heart — love
horse — ambition fulfilled
ladder — advancement

letters — initials of people's names
tree — good luck
ring — marriage
pig — fertility
house, castle — woman
butterfly — pleasures
knife — trouble

numbers
one — freedom, independence
two — second chance
three — journeys and meetings
four — security
five — love
six — fitness
seven — firm friendships
eight — change
nine — unexpected good fortune

The rim of the cup represents the immediate future, the centre of the cup the distant future. The handle represents home. The further a symbol is from the handle the more distant its effect.

'And true love-knots lurked in the bottom of every tea-cup'.

Bibliography

Baildon, S., *Tea Industry in India* (W.H. Allen, London, 1863)

The Fabian Society, *Britain's Food Supplies in Peace and War* (Routledge, London, 1940)

FAO/UNESCO/WMO, *A Study of the Agroclimatology of the Highlands of Eastern Africa*

Forrest, D., *A Hundred Years of Ceylon Tea: 1867–1967* (Chatto and Windus, London, 1967)

Forrest, D., *Tea for the British* (Chatto and Windus, London, 1973)

Fortune, R., *Two Visits to the Tea Countries of China and British Tea Plantations in the Himalayas* (Murray, London, 1857)

Gardner, B., *The East India Company: A History* (Rupert Hart-Davis, London, 1971)

Griffiths, Sir P., *A History of the India Tea Industry* (Weidenfeld and Nicolson, London, 1967)

Honey, W.B., *European Ceramic Art: End of Middle Ages to about 1815* (Faber, London, 1959)

Honey, W.B., *German Porcelain* (Faber, London, 1957)

Huxley, G., *Talking of Tea* (Thames and Hudson, London, 1956)

Money, Lt-Col. E., *Tea and Cultivation* (Whittingham, London, 1870)

Nassau-Lees, W., *Tea Cultivation and Other Agricultural Experiments in India* (W.H. Allen, London, 1863)

Okakura-Kabuzo, *The Book of Tea* (Tuttle, Rutland, Vt., 1956)

Sansom, G.B., *Japan: A Short Cultural History* (Tuttle, Rutland, Vt., 1931)

Sen Soshitsu, *Chanoyu* (Urasenke Foundation, Tokyo, 1970)

Pike, M., *Food and Society* (Murray, London, 1971)

Trevelyan, G.M., *Illustrated English Social History* (Longmans, London, 1951)

Index

Page references in **bold type** refer to pictures.

Other books available from Whittet Books Ltd

The Quest for Paradise: Ronald King

With an Introduction by Anthony Huxley

291 colour, 95 black and white illustrations; 288 pages; hardback £9.95

A world-wide survey of man as gardener, written by the ex-Secretary of Kew Gardens.

The Reluctant Motor Mechanic: John Fordham

120 line drawings; 192 pages; hardback £4.95; paperback £2.95

An approachable guide to the workings of the motor car, and how to cure its ailments.

The Narrow Boat Book: Tom Chaplin

223 illustrations; 128 pages; hardback £7.95; paperback £4.95

The complete, illustrated history of the narrow boat.
'Tom Chaplin does have something to say and he says it well'
– Canal and Riverboat Monthly

H.M. Bateman on Golf

80 pages; hardback £1.75

H.M. Bateman on Music

64 pages; hardback £1.50

Two volumes by the master, selected by theme.

An Autobiographical Novel: Kenneth Rexroth

388 pages; hardback £6.50; paperback £2.95

The fascinating autobiography of poet and translator Kenneth Rexroth.
'. . . a fine book, illuminating both about the author and the period in which he grew up' – *The Times Literary Supplement*

If you would like to purchase any of these titles, please send cheque or postal order, together with 50p per title for postage and packing to: Whittet Books Ltd, The Oil Mills, Weybridge, Surrey